POSTMORTEM CHANGE IN
HUMAN AND ANIMAL REMAINS

POSTMORTEM CHANGE IN HUMAN AND ANIMAL REMAINS

A Systematic Approach

By

MARC S. MICOZZI, M.D., PH.D.

Director, National Museum of Health and Medicine
Associate Director, Armed Forces Institute of Pathology
Washington, D.C.

CHARLES C THOMAS • PUBLISHER
Springfield • Illinois • U.S.A.

Published and Distributed Throughout the World by

CHARLES C THOMAS • PUBLISHER
2600 South First Street
Springfield, Illinois 62794-9265

© *1991 by* CHARLES C THOMAS • PUBLISHER
ISBN 0-398-05747-8
Library of Congress Catalog Card Number: 91-18789

Printed in the United States of America
SC-R-3

Library of Congress Cataloging-in-Publication Data

Micozzi, Marc S., 1953–
    Postmortem change in human and animal remains : a systematic
approach / by Marc S. Micozzi.
        p. cm.
    Includes bibliographical references and index.
    ISBN 0-398-05747-8
    1. Archaeology—Methodology. 2. Animal remains (Archaeology)
3. Anthropometry. 4. Postmortem changes. 5. Taphonomy. I. Title.
CC75.7.M53 1991
930.1′028′5—dc20   91-18789
                                                               CIP

PREFACE

The identification of questions to be asked in science must be tempered by the availability of the means to answer them. Taphonomy has developed as a potentially powerful tool for providing increased means for answering questions about postmortem change. Little has appeared in the forensic medical or anthropological literature concerning postmortem change and time interval since death (Bass 1984). Stewart (1979; 71) devotes less than eight pages out of 300 for determining time since death stating "there is no escaping the fact that for most skeletonized remains, estimation of time since death usually is little more than an educated guess." Other forensic anthropology texts devote less space to determining time since death (Krogman, 1962; El-Najjar and McWilliams, 1978; Krogman and Iscan, 1985; Ubelaker, 1989). In the meantime, an extensive literature on taphonomy has developed in archaeology from historical observations and modern experimental approaches.

An underlying assumption of science is an entropic or centripetal bias in that most natural forces are regarded to tend towards disorganization ("things fly apart," or fall apart). Archaeologic theory continually seeks explanations for why things come together. Taphonomy may be regarded as the study of entropic forces which disorder material remains, cause disturbance of the archaeologic record, and to some extent homogenize material features.

However, these taphonomic transformations are patterned based upon underlying physical, chemical and biological principles. Thus, known patterns for the behavior of remains through taphonomic transformations may lead to information gains, rather than losses, in the archaeologic record.

Postmortem modification and transformation of human and animal remains is determined by the taphonomic principles which govern behavior of all material in the archaeologic record. An approximate chronologic order of the action of taphonomic factors on human and animal remains is given in this book. Taphonomic transformation that occurs early in the postmortem depositional history of remains necessarily conditions the characteristics of changes which come after. The order of operation of taphonomic factors may also vary somewhat within well-defined ranges.

Applications of the taphonomy of organic remains may be found in paleopathology, bioarchaeology, physical anthropology, paleontology, faunal analysis, and historical archaeology and forensic medicine.

CONTENTS

LIST OF TABLES

xi

POSTMORTEM CHANGE IN
HUMAN AND ANIMAL REMAINS

Chapter I

INTRODUCTION: TAPHONOMY IN
THE STUDY OF POSTMORTEM REMAINS

SCOPE OF TAPHONOMY

Taphonomy may be described as the "transferral of organic remains from the biosphere to the lithosphere" (Olson, 1962). The term *taphonomy* was coined by the Russian paleontologist, I.A. Efremov (1940), from the Greek words for tomb or burial (taphos) and for law or system of laws (nomos), to denote a subdiscipline of paleontology devoted to study of the processes that operate on organic remains after death to generate archaeologic skeletal deposits. Postmortem processes affecting organic remains were divided by Muller (1951) into two types of taphonomic transformations: biostratinomic and diagenetic. Biostratinomic processes, first coined by Weigelt (1927), includes all taphonomic transformations from death through burial of remains. Diagenetic processes deal with transformation in soil of organic material to mineral, or fossilization. Biostratinomic processes have been investigated for invertebrate, vertebrate and hominid remains in several early studies, as shown in Table 1. Bone modification and attrition (alteration within primary site) and destruction and transport (disappearance from primary site) are within the biostratinomic realm from death to final burial. Differential responses of bones to these processes relate to biologic as well as taphonomic factors.

Three types of biologic "assemblages" are important with respect to taphonomy: (1) biocoenose is the assemblage of living organisms, (2) thanatocoenose is the assemblage of organisms associated through death, and (3) taphocoenose is the assemblage of organisms localized in an archaeologic context (Voorhies, 1969). Mammals comprise the majority of organic remains studied at hominid sites (Dodson, 1973) and are most relevant to determining patterns of human remains. Grey (1973) has attempted to define the process of deposition of mammalian skeletal assemblages using both biological and geological principles. Grey defines the taphocoenose as a regional association of species in which related,

3

Table 1. Early Studies of Postmortem Processes

Process	Invertebrate	Vertebrate	Human
Disarticulation	N/A	Weigelt (1927) Toots (1965) Clark et al., (1967) Voorhies (1969) Hill (1975, 1976, 1979, 1980)	Dart (1956, 1957) Brain (1967, 1980) Crader (1974)
Transport (aqueous)	Bancot (1953)	Voorhies (1969)	Shipman (1977)
Attrition (weathering)	Craig (1953) Rigby (1958)	Voorhies (1969)	Crader (1974)
Biological Agents (scavenging)		Voorhies (1969) Payne (1965) Sutcliffe (1970)	Hughes (1954, 1958, 1961) Vrba (1975)

site-specific biotic factors (e.g., habitat) and geologic factors (e.g., sedi-mentation patterns) determine the chances for preservation. Death deter-mines the composition of the taphocoenose. Causes of death may be normal attrition (very young and very old) or catastropic (plague, flood, famine, or natural disaster). Average life spans influence relative repre-sentation and accumulation of species. Relative size determines preserva-tion, in that smaller animals are subject to greater destruction during scavenging and burial.

A taphocoenose may be allocthonous (an assemblage arising through transport of remains away from a site) or autochthonous (deposited at the primary site). Thus, skeletal assemblages may be recognized as representing proximal or distal communities, based on place of origin of skeletal elements. The degree of transport of remains is related to their density and degree of disarticulation. An anataxic assemblage is uncovered after burial and again subject to transport and other taphonomic transforma-tions at this stage. The factors influencing human and animal remains postmortem are shown in Table 2.

It may well be considered that the biocoenose is related to biotic factors. Thanatic factors (mortality) result in creation of a thanatocoenose. The composition of a taphocoenose is determined by taphonomic trans-formation in the form of perthotaxic, taphic and anataxic factors. Finally, the validity and reliability of information from skeletal remains are determined by sullegic and trephic factors; what may be referred to as

Table 2. Taphonomic Factors Influencing Human and Animal Remains

Chronology	Factor	Stage	Agents
1	Biotic	(antemortem)	lifestyle, habitat
2	Thanatic	(perimortem)	mortality
3	Perthotaxic	(postmortem, preburial)	predation, scavenging
4	Taphic	(burial)	transport, pedoturbation, diagnesis
5 (return to 3)	Anataxic	(uncovered after burial)	exposure/weathering
6	Sullegic		collecting, sampling
7	Trephic		curatorial

chain of custody in the forensic setting. Taphonomic factors determine the proportion of the target population of an ecosystem, and quantitative and qualitative content of skeletal assemblages, available for study in the archaeologic record. Sampling factors determine what proportion of the study population is in fact studied, and the reliability of that sample for study. Both taphonomic factors and sampling factors enter into the interpretation of human and animal remains postmortem.

Starting Conditions	Agent of Modification	Ending Conditions
Target population	Taphonomic factors	Study population
Study population	Sampling factors	Sample population
Sample population	Statistical factors	Sample fraction

Grayson (1978) has developed indices of number of identified skeletal elements, and number of identified specimens per taxon (NISP) for faunal analysis, which may be useful in taphonomy. He identified several transformational factors and phenomena relevant to taphonomy and sampling:

(1) Dismemberment pattern
(2) Numbers of identified specimens vary from species to species
(3) Usage assumes equal effects of chance on breakage
(4) Differential preservation
(5) Curatorial-collection techniques
(6) Entire skeletons skew abundance

Taphonomy is relevant to points (1), (2), (3) and (4), while sampling is relevant to points (2), (3), (5) and (6).

Taphonomy as a systematic study of postmortem change can be related to traditional forensic pathology in the scheme shown in Table 3 for determination of postmortem time interval. Taphonomy enters into forensic interpretation in Phases III thru V as shown in the table. Phases I and II are not properly in the scope of the present volume. Phase VI generally takes us beyond biological and physical processes of taphonomy into changes that are geologic. However, an understanding of taphonomic processes during Phases III thru V may be important to interpretation of geologic findings.

STUDIES OF POSTMORTEM PROCESSES

Studies of postmortem taphonomic processes have been accomplished by a number of investigators for invertebrate, vertebrate and hominid remains regarding disarticulation, aqueous transport, attrition (weathering) and scavenging (biological agents). Early studies are summarized in Table 1.

Existing studies of postmortem decay and disarticulation have focused on three primary methodologies: (1) observation of naturally-occurring sequences of decay and disarticulation, (2) experimental observation and documentation of decay and disarticulation sequences, and (3) observation of attrition by predators and scavengers to animal remains.

Observational Studies

A number of observations have been made on natural sequences of decay and disarticulation. Weigelt (1927) studied cows on the Gulf Coast of the U.S., and Toots (1975) observed disarticulation sequences in semi-arid regions of Wyoming. Shafer (1978) studied decay and disarticulation sequences of sea birds and mammals in the North Sea and adjacent coastal regions. Completely different criteria and sequences have been proposed by these investigators, and their results are difficult to reconcile. The incompatibility of results seems to be due largely to the wide variety of animals used and conditions under which they were studied. Meaningful generalizations on natural sequences of decay and disarticulation have been difficult to formulate on the basis such observations.

Experimental Studies

Dodson (1973) has carried out experimental observations of decay and disarticulation in small mammals, reptiles and amphibians in the laboratory. The applicability of this work on microfauna to megafaunal and human remains is unclear. Two painstaking studies were conducted

Table 3. Relation of Taphonomy to Traditional Determinations of Postmortem Interval

Time Interval*	Observational Phenomena	Methodology
I. Minutes to Hours	Enzymatic changes cellular respiration	Biochemistry, Cell Biology (e.g., "Chemistry of Death")
II. Hours to One Day	"Classic Triad" algor/livor/rigor mortis (taken together)	Traditional Forensic Pathology
III. One Day–One Week	Gross postmortem decomposition (ocular changes-special case)	Forensic Pathology, Ecology, Taphonomy
IV. Weeks–Months	Disarticulation/skeletonization	Anthropology, Taphonomy, Archaeology
V. Months–Years	Weathering/Burial/Pedoturbation	Taphonomy, Archaeology, Paleoecology
VI. Years–Eons	Fossilization/Diagnesis/Trace Elements	Archaeology, Paleontology, Minerology

*All depend upon environmental conditions, which generally (except at extremes) alter rates, but not types, of process.

on arthropod populations and succession sequences in decaying animals (Payne, 1965; Johnson, 1975). However, both studies used animals which had been previously frozen, and the extent to which decay processes in previously-frozen tissue duplicates the behavior of fresh tissue is questionable (Micozzi, 1986). Furthermore, many animals used were dead at birth, or crushed to death by the mother after birth, with unknown effects on decay and disarticulation patterns which were not controlled.

Payne (1965) also attempted studies of dogs, cats, squirrels, rabbits, chickens, birds and pigs, and concluded that relatively large animals of uniform size were best for experimental study. The presence of feathers on an animal makes the assessment of patterns difficult. He also emphasized thorough and frequent examinations of remains to ensure adequate methodology. There are some discrepencies in the staging of experimental studies. While Payne (1965) determined five or six stages of decay, Johnson (1975) found four stages, similar to Reed (1958) in an earlier study.

Anecdotal Studies

Observations of damage by predators or scavengers to animal remains are largely anecdotal. Few actual reports of observations of pedation or scavenging behavior by carnivores exist in the literature. Einarson (1971) made a rather speculative attempt to describe uniquely-identifying, species-specific consumption patterns for game-bird predators. Galdikas-Brindamour's (1978) study of the scavenging of orangutan (*Pongo pygmaeas*) remains by the Bornean bearded pig (*Sus barbatus*) is interesting, but necessarily anecdotal.

Systematic changes which occur to human and animal remains postmortem, as well as natural and cultural processes which result in preservation of remains, are presented in the remainder of this volume.

Chapter II

POSTMORTEM PRESERVATION AND
MODIFICATION OF SOFT TISSUES:
NATURAL PROCESSES

S oft tissue remains are usually subject to a combination of cultural processes, biological agents and natural transformations, which may include dismemberment, predation and scavenging, and putrefaction and decay. Thus, most human and animal remains enter the archaeologic record as bone, and most bone in the archaeologic record is disarticulated. However, natural and artificial processes of desiccation may lead to mummification with partial or total preservation of soft tissue. Immediate postmortem change is essentially a competition between decay and desiccation, and external factors such as temperature and humidity largely determine the outcome of this contest (Aufderheide, 1981; Micozzi, 1986). Natural preservation of soft tissues after death may occur through desiccation (drying), freezing and sublimation (freeze-drying) and fixation by mineral salts (nitre, natron, salt peter), mineralized water, tannic acids, or other chemicals.

Hot, dry climatological conditions favor dessication in many parts of the world, including the coastal zones of Chile and Peru, the canyons of the southwestern United States and northern Mexico, and especially the deserts of Australia and North Africa (as in Egypt). Preservation of soft tissue also occurs with freezing through a process of sublimation, or freeze-drying, in regions within the Artic and Antarctic circles, and at high altitude, and with natural processes of fixation by mineral salts and tannic acid.

Gifford (1981) describes the ideal conditions for preservation of organic remains as "very wet or very dry," with relatively rapid burial. Favorable climatological and environmental conditions alternatively include dry, hot sands; a cold or cool climate; and airtight water seals. Binford (1981) describes ideal conditions for preservation as quick burial with perpetuation of natural moisture content, or alternatively, complete desiccation.

9

The activity of biological agents causing postmortem modification is discussed vis-á-vis these empirical features of preservation.

Human skin is well preserved by drying, boiling or smoking, as seen in American Indian scalps, shrunken heads, and bodies buried in dry sand. Burned or smoked skin does not decompose due to inhibition of bacterial growth (Baden, 1982; Saul and Micozzi, 1988, 1989) (see Chap. V). The pre-dynastic mummies of ancient Egypt demonstrate excellent preservation of the epidermis after burial in shallow, dry-sand graves for thousands of years (Giacometti and Chiarelli, 1968; Daniels and Post, 1970). Some processes of natural preservation, as in fixation by tannic acid in the Danish "Bog people," may result in preservation of skin only (Aufderheide, 1981).

PRESERVATION BY DESICCATION

Rapid drying of soft tissues prevents putrefaction by enteric micro-organisms, soil bacteria and other decay organisms. Mummies of the Amerindian tribes of the American Southwest were preserved primarily due to the hot, dry climate and desiccatory effects of the sands in which they were buried. Prehistoric mummies from the Basket-maker culture were found tightly wrapped in blankets, and bodies as well as woven clothing and textiles were well preserved (Guernsey and Kidder, 1919). Soft tissue preservation was sufficient to permit anatomic diagnosis in cases recently examined (Aufderheide, 1980; El-Najjar and Mulinski, 1980).

PRESERVATION BY SALT

Preservation may also be accomplished by exposure to mineral salts due to their affinity for moisture and desiccatory effects on soft tissue.

Mummies have been found in Mammoth Cave, Kentucky, preserved due to the niter content of the cave, and in the saltpeter caves of the Lower Mimbres Valley in southern New Mexico (Fawkes, 1914). There are similarly preserved mummies throughout the Eastern United States, where many Amerindian tribes buried their dead in caves (Maloney, 1981).

PRESERVATION IN WATER

Soft tissues may be partially preserved in water when there is an airtight seal. Paleo-Indian remains were discovered in a flooded sink-hole in southwest Florida dating from 10,000 to 4,000 B.C. Brain tissues, as well as skeletal materials, from an estimated 1,000 human burials were found. Preservation was attributed to creation of an anaerobic environment by mineralized hard water and resettling of fine peat (Clausen et al., 1979). This aquatic environment allowed preservation of a vast array of human remains, vertebrate and invertebrate fossils, and artifacts of wood, shell, bone and soft tissue which seldom survive in the American Southeast. Mineralized water with a salinity of 3.2 per mil, average temperature of 24.4° C and 0 (zero) dissolved oxygen, flows from the cavity at a rate of 42.8 liters per second. This weak flow of mineralized water is apparently a relatively recent phenomenon linked to present sea level. In the past, during periods of lower local ground water level, the sinkhole was a freshwater cenote.

Brain tissue has also been found to be preserved due to the formation of adipocere (Tkocz et at., 1979). Adipocere had been thought to result from chemical saponification of organic fatty acids in the presence of alkali (e.g., lime or calcium carbonate). Adipocere is now thought to consist primarily of fatty acids formed by the postmortem hydrolysis and hydrogenation of body fats (Mant and Furbank, 1957). This process is observed to be more common in females due to the greater average body fat deposition. It was previously thought that extraneous water was needed for the process (Evans, 1963a:ch. 7). However, adipocere formation has been observed to occur after long inhumation under relatively dry conditions (Evans, 1963b). Pre-inhumation conditions of warm weather, fog or haze are regarded to contribute to the process (Evans, 1963a:ch. 7). Preservation of human tissue has been observed after immersion in freshwater for five years (Cotton, Aufderheide, Goldschmidt, 1987).

PRESERVATION BY FIXATION

Preservation of soft tissue has been observed due to the action of tannic acid in peat bogs, also found in tea. Preserved "Bog people" have been found in Northern Europe dating to the Danish Iron Age, 400 B.C. to A.D. 400 (Glob, 1969). The preservation of such cases as "Tollund man," "Windeby girl," "Gruballe man," "Lindow Man" (Stead, Bourke, Brothwell, 1986) and those in the Haraldskjaer Bog, is attributed to activity by bog acids which decalcify bone and tan skin, as well as maintaining an anaerobic aquatic environment. Most of these cases were victims of human sacrifice, showing evidence of blunt trauma, strangulation, drowning, torture, dismemberment and/or cutting of the throat, with multiple traumatic fractures. The skin in these cases is better preserved than are the internal viscera (Aufderheide, 1981). Extreme demineralization with decalcification of bones is an important characteristic of this type of preservation (Stead, Bourke, Brothwell, 1986). The preservative effects of tannic acid were known to Shakespeare's Hamlet, who asks in his preoccupation with paternal postmortem appearance(s), how long it takes for the bones to lose flesh. He is told, "seven years, longer for tanners," exposed to tannic acid during life.

PRESERVATION BY FREEZING

Soft tissue preservation has been observed due to freezing in Scythian bodies from Middle East permafrost zones (Artamanov, 1965). Scythian tombs in the Altai Mountains of Siberia were found to contain well-preserved human remains (Rudenko, 1970). Herodotus (IV:66–71) provides an early description of Scythian burial practices at the death of a king, who was eviscerated, mummified, entombed and covered by stone cairns.

Several frozen Siberian woolly mammoths (*Mammuthus primigenius*) have been well preserved, well studied and are well known (e.g., Goodman et al., 1980).

Soft tissues have also been preserved through freezing in circumpolar areas of North America, during ancient and more recent times. A frozen, mummified body, complete with tatoos, was found on St. Lawrence Island, Alaska, dating from 400 B.C. (Smith and Zimmermann, 1975). The body of arctic explorer Charles Francis Hall, who died of arsenic poisoning and was buried in 1871 at Thank-God-Harbour, Greenland, was exhumed and autopsied on site in 1968, with good preservation of soft tissue (Horne, 1980). The preservative potential of arsenic itself is also noted, as in the case of Elmer McCurdy, a turn-of-the-century Western outlaw, embalmed with arsenic and preserved for a carnival show.

Soft tissue preservation under conditions of freezing is potentially ideal, but the practical limitations of discovery conditions often preclude examination prior to the onset of post-recovery deterioration (Aufderheide, 1981). Further, exposure of soft tissues to alternate freeze-thaw cycles with time also introduces confounding variables (Micozzi, 1986). Depending upon latitude, season of death and stratigraphy of placement in the ground, animal and human remains may be subjected to freezing with or without subsequent thaw. Wood and Johnson (1978) have illustrated zones of continuous and discontinuous permafrost worldwide, and maximum depths of frost penetration in seasonally frozen ground in the United States (Chapter VII).

Chapter III

POSTMORTEM PRESERVATION AND MODIFICATION OF SOFT TISSUES: CULTURAL PROCESSES

Beliefs and practices surrounding death, dying, burial and handling of the dead have profound effects on the final deposition of human remains. Cultural characteristics of burial, cremation, embalming, entombment, internment, mortuary practices and public health all influence the disposition of human remains. Beliefs about death and dying influence the treatment and handling of human remains, and structure and pattern their deposition, for all members of a society. Mortuary practices may be more specifically determined by social identity of the individual undergoing burial, which may appear in the archaeologic record on this basis (Tainter, 1978). In oral cultures, the funeral is seen to sum up the past history as well as the social relations of the deceased (Kopytoff, 1971). Figure 1 shows the different ways in which various cultures handle disposition of human remains.

It is possible to determine how belief systems surrounding death and dying influence the archaeologic record. Conversely, cognitive archaeology seeks to determine patterns of thought and belief systems from the archaeologic record (Gould, 1978). The anthropology of human residue formation may also be related to non-material or ideational aspects of behavior (the "ideotechnic" meaning of archaeologic material) (Binford, 1962). The search for "deep structures" in discard behavior may help reveal universal human patterns of cognition which may be codified. Ethnoarchaeologic documentation of the flow of durable elements and consumable products through a systemic context may yield insights into the relationship between material culture and symbols, cognition, values and beliefs (Gould, 1978).

Cultural information can be revealed by patterns in the archaeologic record through conceptual attributes of ideology in a society. The organizational attributes of a society may also be revealed in internment

15

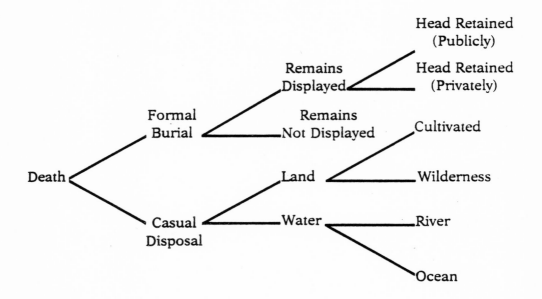

Figure 1. Cultural approaches to disposition of human remains. (Drawn from Tainter, 1978).

practices (Stannard, 1975). Emile Durkheim, Robert Hertz and Jack Goody have all written on death and the interpretation of culture, and Clifford Geertz has described how the ethos of death may reveal the world view of a culture (Stannard, 1977). Bronislow Malinowski, Herbert Spencer and E. B. Tylor have all indicated that human burials in the Upper Paleolithic suggest the existence of a symbolic and ideologic "halo" surrounding the facts of death (e.g., red ochre, burial positions, and funerary rituals). The extent to which synchronic beliefs about death relate to long-term diachronic perspectives is debatable (Aries, 1974). V. Gordon Childe (1956) has described the occurence through time of extravagant funeral customs during periods of political instability (Stannard, 1977). Sir James Frazier (*The Golden Bough*) early described fear of the dead in many cultures, which may be based upon considerations of hygiene, as with the Hebrew dietary laws (Feldman, 1977). Aries (1974) has described the need to "tame" death, as well as the importance of mourning. Lack of mourning leads to deprivation of the death experience.

Enrich Lindemann described the difficulty experienced in adjusting to the death of relatives killed in the Coconut Grove fire in Boston, without an opportunity for viewing the body. Viewing the body provides powerful visual imagery. Historical mummification practices were partially an attempt to preserve remains for some to allow the mourning process to continue, even where climatologic factors required eventual internment or cremation.

Human remains, with or without preservation of soft tissue, are rarely deposited into the archaeologic record unaltered by human hands. Postmortem modification of deceased members of a society is an almost intrinsic characteristic of human culture. During the Paleolithic Period, deceased humans were painted with red ochre, "the ruddy coloring of life in an attempt to make the body usable for its owner" (Macalister, 1921).

Postmortem modification of human remains by other humans is intrinsic to many cultures, both diachronically and synchronically, and must be taken into account for effects on the deposition and appearance of soft tissues and skeletal remains in the archaeologic record.

Knowledge of the cultural processes which are likely to be superimposed upon natural processes are useful in understanding ultimate patterns of deposition and differential survival of human remains. Cultural processes of postmortem transformation range from complete or partial preservation, as with artificial mummification, to outright destruction.

Mummification

The term *mummification* refers to all natural and artificial processes that bring about preservation of the body or its parts. Such methods include drying by air, sun, or fire (with or without evisceration), covering with plastic material (such as clay), filling body cavities with plant or other materials, and embalming with chemical or other substances.

There are three principal types of mummification: (1) *natural mummification,* caused by a number of factors singly or in combination, such as dryness, heat, cold, or absence of air in the burial vault or grave; (2) *intentional mummification,* brought about by intentional exploitation or deliberate enhancement of the natural processes listed above; and (3) *artifical mummification,* produced by a variety of techniques including evisceration, fire and smoke curing, and application of embalming substances such as resin, oils, herbs, and other organic materials and chemicals. In pre-Columbian South America only natural and intentional mummification were employed, while in Ancient Egypt mummification processes ranged from natural to artificial during the dynastic periods.

The word *mummy* is derived from the Persian *mumeia* or *mum*, meaning pitch or asphalt. This substance had been used in classical times in medical prescriptions, but medieval physicians introduced a refinement with preparations of pitch from Egyptian mummies. These "exudations" of mummies became very popular and remained so up to the nineteenth century. The first use of the word referring to medicine dates back to the early fifteenth century (Encyclopedia Britannica, 1911). As applied to a preserved body, however, the earliest record is 1615 (Oxford English Dictionary).

Artificial mummification, specifically, and other forms of soft tissue preservation, have been practiced by various cultural groups around the world through time. The cultural roots of artificial mummification lie in beliefs about life after death. It is generally acknowledged that techniques of artificial mummification and preservation are effective only in those regions in which climatological conditions favor natural preservation. It is also hypothesized that in those regions where natural mummification occurred (with early opportunity for observation of natural mummies) human cultures developed notions of the possible utility of the body after death, and became duly motivated to develop artificial procedures for the preservation of soft tissues. In ancient Egypt, decay was observed when bodies were no longer placed in natural sand graves; and cultural practices, such as evisceration and desiccation, were adopted to minimize these postmortem changes. In areas where long-term preservation of human tissues was precluded due to unfavorable environmental conditions, efforts at artificial mummification were undertaken to facilitate short-term preservation only. Common features of artificial mummification include evisceration to prevent intrinsic decay processes due to enteric micro-organisms, and desiccation through sun exposure, air drying, salt treatment or smoking.

Postmortem patterns of modification to human remains during mummification rituals and processes are of interest to archaeologists and paleopathologists in obtaining contextual information from such remains. A brief survey of cultural practices of artificial mummification is undertaken to elucidate the scope of possible modifications ranging from soft tissue preservation to destruction, as detectable in the archaeologic record. The oldest known artificial mummy is that of Menkhara, third king of the Egyptian Fourth Dynasty (ca. 4000 B.C.), now in the British Museum (Elliot-Smith and Dawson, 1924). Postmortem modification has since been practiced in Ancient Egypt, Greece and Rome; by the ancient

Hebrews, Babylonians, Persians and Indians; in the islands of the Pacific, Torres Straits and Australia; in Burma and Ceylon; on the southwest and west coasts of Africa and the Canary Islands; and in the New World by Amerindian tribes from Virginia to Florida, and by Incas in Argentina, Bolivia, Chile and Peru.

NORTH AMERICA

Several prehistoric Amerindian tribes practiced various forms of post-mortem modification and preservation.

The Hopi placed their dead in a squatting or fetal position and wrapped them in mats (Malefijt, 1969). The Basket-maker culture of prehistoric Arizona (A.D. 100–700) wrapped the dead in woven mats of fur and yucca fiber. In the Lower Mimbres Valley, southern New Mexico, the deceased were packed in red clay and a large perforated plate was placed over the face (Fawkes, 1914). These human remains placed in the dry, hot southwestern United States were all preserved through the operation of natural desiccation.

On the East Coast, Amerindians practiced more active techniques. In Virginia, Indian chiefs were skinned and fleshed, with soft tissue removed and bones bleached (Stewart, 1978). The bones were then replaced in the skin, and the body was packed with white sand and rubbed with oil. In Florida, remains were smoked for preservation and buried in caves.

The Aleutian and Kodiak Indians had the most developed techniques of artificial mummification in North America. Evisceration was carried out through the pelvis and the body was exposed to solar desiccation. Dried grass and moss was used for embalming and the body was stuffed with straw (Dall, 1978). Fingernails and eyes were often removed. The body was then placed in a fixed position and wrapped, or dressed and posed in a natural position (James, 1957). In the Unalaska District, burial was carried out in a painted wooden coffin (March, 1937). The practices and the resulting mummies were carefully examined during the Stoll-McCracken Expedition of the 1930s (Lantis, 1971).

An example of a destructive technique of postmortem modification is provided by the Diegueños of Southern California, who dressed their dead in effigial wrappings and burned them after one week of mourning (Contributions to North American Enthology, 1887).

CENTRAL AND SOUTH AMERICA

In pre-Columbian South America preservation was based primarily upon the desiccatory effects of dry sand and heat.

Mummification in South America dates back to historic practices in ancient Chile among the Chinchorro (6000–3000 B.C.). Unburied, the Chinchorro mummies stood erect as statues, propped up among the living. In southern Peru, during the Chavin Period (1200 B.C.–A.D. 400) in the deserts of Nazca and on the plains of Ica, mummies were wrapped in a "fardo," or caricature of the deceased (Waisbard and Waisbard, 1965). In the Walla tribe of pre-Inca Peru, the "fardo" was depicted with large eyes, while the Mochica-Chimu and Nazca fardos had almond-shaped eyes, although the latter rarely practiced mummification. The mummies were then buried in structures used as temples, as well as tombs. This practice spread during the Tiahuanaco Period. In northern Peru, the dead had been wrapped in woven reed mats, or "barbacoases," and buried in the sand for dessication, until contact with the Tiahuanaco (Vreeland, 1978).

Not much is known about mummification in South America from the advent of the Inca Empire in A.D. 1200 to the Spanish Conquest in 1578. The mummies of Inca rulers were kept at the Temple of the Sun in Cuzco, brought out for special occasions, periodically reclothed and borne on stretchers, as during the November "Festival of the Dead" described by Guaman Poma in 1613 (1956). With the arrival of Francisco Pizarro, and the Spanish Conquest of 1578, many royal Inca mummies were burned as idolatry, representing an early "curatorial" loss of theretofor preserved human remains, and the Incas discontinued the practice. The Mayans and Aztecs also practiced mummification to a limited extent, with mummified jaguar remains found in one royal Mayan burial (Sharer and Ashmore, 1979:338).

Although throughout South America preservatives were not primarily used for mummification, and preservation was based on the desiccatory effects of sand and dry heat; freezing may have been a factor in preservation of some mummies, as in the cases of the "Frozen Inca Boy" and a Chilean (and chilly) male found in a female burial (Post and Donner, 1972).

Mummification was also practiced by the Huarochiri and Youyos Indians of South America. When the Spanish first entered Northern Peru and Ecuador during 1531–1535, they discovered a culture in which the bodies of the dead were flayed to remove soft tissues from underlying bone. The heads were shrunken and mummified in a process similar to that employed by the Jivaro Indians until the twentieth century. The Jivaro Indians of the Cordillera de Cutucu in the Upper Amazon River Basin of southeastern Ecuador are responsible for the preparation of the well known *tsanta,* or "shrunken heads." The process consisted of removal of the scalp, flaying of the soft tissue of the head and removal of the bones of the skull. The skin was shrunk to approximately half original size by air drying, then boiled in hinto juice (rich in natural tannins) and dried on a spear shaft. The apertures of the nostrils and orbits were sewn together and the hair tied back with plant fibers. The head was then filled with hot sand, continually replaced as it cooled. The head was preserved on the external surface by the continual application of heated pebbles, vegetable oils, plant extracts, and powdered charcoal, serving to darken the color. The final result of this process is known as a "tsanta" (McHargue, 1972). The tanning process resulted in good preservation of skin despite the unfavorable climatological conditions of the Amazon Basin.

ASIA

In Tibet, there has traditionally been prompt disposal of the bodies of most deceased due to limited availability of arable land for cultivation. Further, there is little wood for funeral pyres and both Bhuddist doctrine and the granite earth prohibit the digging of graves. Dead bodies are flayed and dismembered, with bones cracked and skulls crushed, and fed to carrion birds. This traditional practice is carried on today by members of a special caste (Allman, 1981). However, some mummification is practiced in Tibet for noblemen, with bodies stored in special containers resembling small Bhuddist temples (Lips, 1947).

Parsis, followers of the Persian prophet Zoroaster (Zarathustra), believe that burial or cremation of the dead defiles the sacred elements of earth, fire and water. In Bombay, where the largest colony of Parsis resides, there is an enclosure on Malabar Hill where the dead are placed to be consumed by vultures (Naipaul, 1981).

The ancient Persians and Scythians used wax and fungi, as well as salt, niter, cedar, balsam and gypsum, in preservation of mummies. The ancient Babylonians also made use of honey, which may function as a natural antibacterial agent (see Chap. IV). By contrast, the Ainu of

Hokkaido, Japan, eviscerate their dead and desiccate them in the sun (James, 1957).

In Southeast Asia, climatological conditions preclude tissue preservation in most circumstances. Many of the tribes of the Indonesian islands initially mummify the dead but later burn or bury the bodies (McHargue, 1972). A description of a jar burial site in the Philippine Islands emphasized poor preservation of bones and burial materials due to climatological and soil conditions (Guthe, 1937), which also pertain throughout most of insular Southeast Asia. In tropical regions, plants grow rapidly and roots readily destroy any tissue within reach (Warren, 1975, 1980).

In retracing the historic voyage of Alfred Russel Wallace (1869) through the Indonesian archipelago, Lawrence and Lorne Blair (1988) documented the burial practices on several of the archipelago's thousands of islands, which include postmortem mummification and preservation. In the fiefdom of Pau in East Sumba, the dead are placed squatting upright with elbows on knees and palms on cheeks, wrapped in intricate woven textiles. The body is attended by two young boys who keep flies and insects away, and may remain in this condition for twenty years or more before burial. A four-ton megalith is then raised to honor the dead.

Elsewhere, among the Toraja of the Celebes (Sulawesi) highlands, entire villages of three-story houses built like "space arcs" are erected specifically for the funeral of a noble and torn down afterward. A death-house sits in the center of the funeral village, where the body awaits final rites, wrapped in red velvet embroidery with a bamboo pipe beneath to drain postmortem fluids into a Ming porcelain bowl. Formerly the ancestral skeletonized remains were tended by child descendents with the cleaned skulls and femurs arranged neatly in piles.

The current Toraja custom of burying the dead in high vaults in the cliffs began only a few hundred years ago when Bugis pirates (the bogey man of western lore) began pillaging burial sites for the grave goods interred with the bodies. Life-size Tau-Tau's, carved in the likeness of the dead, are dressed in their clothes and placed on the balconies of the Toraja death-cliffs. Surrounded by the balconies of the Tau-Tau's, the bodies of the dead lie in rectangular vaults hollowed out of the rock.

The head-hunting Dyaks of Borneo in Indonesia maintain a house in the center of the village in an upper story of which captured heads are kept and suspended by a string which passes through a perforation in the top of the skull (Gillman, 1875: 238).

WESTERN PACIFIC

Most cultures of the Western Pacific preserved their mummies through drying and smoking. The body was often decapitated. Burials are notable for an absence of grave goods.

Under prevailing climatic conditions, most mummification processes were unsuccessful at permanent preservation, so that preservation for short-term mourning periods was sought, and mummified remains were later burned or buried. The peoples of Samoa, Tonga, San Cristobal and the Gilbert Islands mummified their dead and kept them in the households for a limited time, similar to some Indonesian practices. The goal of mummification in these instances was one of short-term preservation only, with eventual discard of postcranial remains, and frequent retention of decapitated heads.

In 1768, Captain Cook first reported the practice of mummification in Tahiti. The body of the deceased was desiccated on a platform, and pressed to remove fluids. Occcasionally, brains and viscera were removed and the abdominal cavity stuffed with perfumed bark cloth (Rivers, 1927). The head was often severed after a period of time and the body buried (James, 1957).

The Mangaia mummified all dead by desiccation, rubbing with oil and wrapping in bark cloth (tapa or kapa) without evisceration. The body was then buried in a cave, removed periodically and the mummification process was repeated (Hongi, 1916).

The Maori of New Zealand desiccated and smoked the deceased bodies of their chiefs. The brain was removed and the body fluids and abdominal contents drained through the anus (McHargue, 1972). Heads were severed and separately preserved by smoking (James, 1957). The Papuans of New Guinea also decapitated the head, which was desiccated, and the face was reconstructed (Hamlyn-Harris, 1913). The Ladrones also kept only the heads of the deceased (Hawkesworth, 1774).

In the Torres Strait, mummies were preserved by dessication and evisceration. The brain was removed through the cribriform plate of the ethmoid bone (Elkin, 1953). The Papuan mummification process and concomitant cultural practices were felt to be indigenous, thus having refuting Elliot-Smith's early concept of diffusion from Egypt (Petty, 1969).

The Eastern Australian aborigines practiced mummification with evisceration (Service, 1958). The hair was cut from the head, the body rubbed with oil, and the skin punctured with needles to facilitate desiccation. After two months drying time, the hair was reattached, the abdomen filled with tapa (bark cloth) and the body clothed for burial.

By contrast, in another process, the body of the chief was flayed, with flesh removed, desiccated and rolled in woven mats. The skeleton was then sewn back into the skin and placed on a guarded platform (Birket-Smith, 1957). The Munkan of Australia mummified all their dead and then cremated them (McConnel, 1957).

SUB-SAHARAN AFRICA

Postmortem modification of human remains in Sub Saharan Africa has great antiquity. Herodotus (III:22–25) describes Ethiopian burial customs including desiccation by the "Egyptian process," as well as others. The body was enclosed in a shaft of mineral "crystal" and preserved in the household for one year, without noticeable decay. The ancient Ugandans eviscerated the deceased and washed the bodies in beer (hops is thought to have an antibacterial effect). The body fluids were removed with sponges and the viscera replaced. The body was then rubbed with animal butter and wrapped in bark cloth. The fluid by-products were consumed by wives and slaves (Murdock, 1934). The head was often severed after embalming, and retained.

The Babwende of the Congo also practiced ritual mummification and hung bodies from the roof for purposes of desiccation. The Bantu smoked the body in smoldering ashes, wrapped it in cloth and buried it (Lips, 1947). Preservation of mummies from the Canary Islands, off the west coast of Africa, is generally thought to be not as good as that of Egyptian mummies (Brothwell et al., 1969).

ANCIENT EGYPT

More information is available on mummification practices in ancient Egypt than for the rest of the world combined, although the Egyptians themselves did not leave behind many writings on mummification (Rowling, 1961). A combination of desiccation and evisceration was generally used to minimize or eliminate sources of postmortem putrefaction and decay.

Herodotus (II:83–91) provides the earliest description of mummification practices in Egypt based upon his travels there during the Late Period, fifth century B.C. (457–453 B.C.). He described three available methods of mummification based upon cost, with or without evisceration, and with or without natron treatment. These three variants essentially represented the earliest discovered to most newly developed techniques. The most recent method at that time dated to the Eighteenth Dynasty. The Romans, Pliny and Diodorus Siculus in 50 B.C. also provided reports on Egyptian mummification. (Rowling, 1961).

Pre-Dynastic Egyptians (4800–3100 B.C.) were buried in shallow sand graves, which manifested the maximum desiccatory effect. These sand pits provided preservation through natural mummification processes. During the later Dynastic Periods (3100–322 B.C.), decay was observed to occur when human remains were subsequently kept from primary contact with desiccating sand by placement in wooden coffins and burial in tombs. Developments in artificial mummification during ensuing dynasties, as summarized in Table 4, were meant to minimize decay. The "secret" of Egyptian mummification lay in (1) removal of soft viscera to minimize internal decomposition, (2) treatment with natural salts (natron) to dry the body, and (3) preservation with resins, oils, spices and other natural products that prevent bacterial growth. With the decline of these practices in the Late Period (XXVI–XXX Dynasties), bodies were usually only wrapped and only skeletons remain today.

Animals that were mummified at one time or another in ancient Egypt include cats, bats, sheep, birds, monkeys, bulls, foxes, cows, fish, crocodiles, and dogs (Elliot Smith and Derry, 1910). The selection of animals buried during a given period in ancient Egypt exhibits marked regional variation (Maloney, 1982).

The materials (Lucas and Harris, 1962) and methods (Evans:CH. 7) of mummification used in formation of the Egyptian archaeologic funerary record have been discussed.

Natron

Mummification in Egypt was characterized by the practice of evisceration, which helped minimize postmortem putrefaction and decay. To facilitate desiccation, natron, an alkaline-mineral-salt mixture was used as a dehydrating agent for the organs and body. Natron (Egyptian *netjery*, Greek *nitron*, chemical symbol Na, for sodium) is naturally-occurring hydrated sodium carbonate ($Na_2CO_31H_2O$) with sodium bicarbonate, sodium chloride, sodium sulfate, natural impurities and other mineral salts. These salts cause chemical decomposition of fatty acids with saponification (Harris and Weeks, 1973).

Natron occurs at three sites in Egypt: in the sand around dry mineral

Table 4. Chronology of Egyptian Mummification Practices

Period & Dynasties	Techniques	Results
Pre-Dynastic (Upper Egypt) 4800–3100 B.C.	Natural mummification. Placed naked or wrapped in woven reed mat or goat skin in shallow grave.	Well preserved
Early Dynastic I–II (Archaic) 3100–2686 B.C.	Limbs wrapped in linen sheets. Bodies placed in coffins.	Poorly preserved, fragile
Old Kingdom III–VI 2686–2181 B.C.	Evisceration (not including brain). Abdominal cavity stuffed with resin, linen; external features covered with strips of linen soaked in resin; use of natural natron solution, aromatic spices	Poorly preserved, fragile
First Intermediate Period VII–X 2181–2050 B.C.	No evidence of mummification.	
Middle Kingdom XI–XII 2050–1750 B.C.	Some evisceration with heart sometimes left in place. Use of dry natron; linen not molded. "Liquid" evisceration; no ventral incision; some brain tissues left in place.	Loosely wrapped, yellow and brittle, or dry, hard and black
Second Intermediate (Hyksos) Period XIII–XVII 1750–1567 B.C.	No evidence of mummification.	
New Kingdom XVIII–XX 1567–1080 B.C.	Brain extracted through nose; heart, kidneys, retroperitoneum left in body; use of heated resin.	Carefully wrapped Thebes: yellow, polished. Memphis: dry, black

Table 4. Continued

Period & Dynasties	Techniques	Results
Late New Kingdom (Nubian) XXI–XXIV 1080–715 B.C.	Evisceration, visceral packets placed in abdomen, use of common salt, first use mud packing.	Well preserved
Late Period (and Saite Period) XXV–XXXI 715–332 B.C.	Head filled with resin Visceral packets placed between legs, outside body.	Poor preservation
Ptolemaic (Greek) Period 332–30 B.C.	No ventral incision or evisceration. Reduced use of resin; no use of natron; use of bitumen.	Sealed bandages heavy and black
Roman Period 30 B.C.–395 A.D.	Renaissance of traditional mummification attempted by Romans as means of "cultural preservation."	Well preserved
Byzantine (Christian) Period 395–641 A.D.	Decline of mummification	
Islamic Period 641 to present	Cessation of mummification	

lakes at Wadi-el-Natron, 70 km west of Cairo in the Libyan Desert; Beheira, Lower Egypt; and Edfu, Upper Egypt. It is found both in the crystalline and liquid states. Lucas (1932) demonstrated that solid natron was used for desiccation of the body, as described by Herodotus (II:83–91). The organs were soaked in 3% natron solution before placement in canopic jars. Later, dry natron was used for organs as well (Harris and Weeks, 1973). Natron artifact to body tissue consists of caustic peeling of the dermis (Dawson, 1927), with hardening of the skin, separation from underlying tissue and loss of hair. The head was not submerged in natron (Dawson, 1927) and the face and head may thus be relatively spared of these effects. Desiccation by means of natron produces a range of tissue weight loss which is characteristically 25 percent (Coughlin, 1977).

The viscera were placed in canopic jars, which were all human headed until the Eighteenth Dynasty, after which they represented the four sons of Horus: Mestha (Amset or Imsety), Hapi (Hapy), Tuamantef (Dua-mutef) and Qebksennuf (see Table 5). Later, the organs were placed in visceral packets and wrapped in the abdominal cavity or placed between the legs.

Resins

Resin was used for preservation of the body after desiccation and is thought to have been poured into the body cavity as a hot liquid, which later cooled. Heated resin kills bacteria and contributes to the creation of an airtight seal. The terms acacia, balsam, pitch, cedar oil and mastic have been applied to solid or semi-solid organic resins obtained directly from certain plants as exudations. These materials were derived from different plant sources in Arabia, Syria (e.g., oak), Lebanon and Punt (Somali coast of Africa). Loss of political control over these geographic areas during the Ptolemaic period, when Egypt was under Macedonian rule, coincides with reduced use of resin in mummification. Hot resin burned the epidermis and subsequent polymerization and setting makes treated tissues difficult to examine and wrappings hard to remove.

An alternative theory for the observed penetration of resins into body cavities is based upon identification of juniper as a primary source of this material (Coughlin, 1977). The constituent obtained from this species is usually considered an oil, rather than a resin (Cockburn and Cockburn, 1980). Tapping the juniper or cedar tree, as is done with pines, yields very little material, and the process for extraction of so-called "cedar-oil" is by steam distillation of wood. This liquid material, as described by Herodotus, and in the Egyptian text, *The Book of the Opening of the Mouth* (James, 1961; Sauneron, 1952), could penetrate into body cavities but would polymerize with time into a hard, resin-like material (Sulzer, 1981). A resin and sawdust mixture was often used to stuff the abdominal cavity, and to seal the bandages after wrapping. The juniper tree resin commonly used by Egyptian embalmers leaves behind a dark pigment that can be detected in joint spaces. This dark pigment has been mistakenly taken as evidence of high prevalance of alkapatonuria in ancient Egyptians, especially since natron treatment enhances the appearance of the pigment on postmortem x-ray (Aufderheide, 1983).

Oils and Spices

Oils and spices were also used in preparation and preservation of soft tissues. Olibanum oil (oil of frankincense) is a corrosive used to dissolve

Table 5. Contents of Canopic Jars

Son of Horus	Depiction	Contents
Imsety (Mestha)	human-headed	liver and gall bladder
Hapy (Hapi)	baboon-headed	lungs (and heart)
Kebehsenuef (Qebeh-senwef)	hawk-headed	small intestines
Dua-Mutef (Tuamautef)	jackal-headed	stomach and large intestines

internal vicera by instillation of the mixture through the anus. A corrosive acidic mixture of juniper or cedar oil, oil of turpentine, and tar was also used in this technique of "liquid evisceration."

The aromatic spices, myrrh, cassia and frankincense, were present in the earliest known mummy dating to the fourth Dynasty. They were characteristically mixed with linens used to stuff the adbominal cavity and wrap viscera. Although the aesthetic qualities of these aromatic perfumes have been emphasized, their possible antibiotic effects should not be discounted. Aromatic oils and spices used in Egyptian mummification are summarized in Table 6. Onions were packed into the head or body or affixed to the feet, a finding reported as early as Granville (1825). The ancient Egyptians used cumin, wax, gum, natron, cedar oil, milk, wine and honey in washing and packing the mummy.

Bitumen (including asphaltum, maltha and gilsonite), a dark-colored, solid substance comprised of hydrocarbons, was used in later mummification processes. Asphaltum and pure bitumen had a preservative action. Curatorial losses of mummified remains have been significant. As rich hydrocarbon sources in a fuel-poor nation, mummies were later used as firewood (particularly those treated with bitumen). They were employed exclusively on the Egyptian Railroad steam engines during its initial ten years of operation. European merchants during the Middle Ages also maintained an active "mummy trade" for medicinal purposes. Mummy wrappings were also used in the Canadian rag industry during the nineteenth century (Cockburn and Cockburn, 1980).

CHEMICAL EMBALMING
DURING THE NINETEENTH CENTURY

Chemical embalming as practiced during the nineteenth century may apparently prevent bacterial decay of soft tissues long enough for preservation to occur. Tissues embalmed with alum may subsequently be

Table 6. Oils and Spices Used in Egyptian Mummification

Material	Compound	Source	Use
Balsam	oleoresins	fragrant exudates of burseraceous trees, *Commiphora* sp.	resins
Cassia	cinnamon	caesalpiniaceous herbs, shrubs, trees, *Cassia sp.*	aromatic
Cedar, pine	pitch, sap crude turpentine	bark of cedar and pine trees	resin
Frankincense	gum resins	*Boswellia sp.*, esp. *B. Carterus* Asia & Africa	aromatic incense
Mastic	astringent resins	anacardiaceous evergreens *Pistacia lentiscus* Mediterranean	aromatic
Myrrh	aromatic exudate	Genus *Commiphora*, esp. *C. myrrha*	incense perfume
Onions	propanethiol S-oxide $(C_6H_6SO) + H_2O$ Sulfuric acid	onion bulbs, stems, roots	stuffed in head or tied to feet

preserved through a process of mummification. The case of Col. William Mabry Shy, CSA, of Tennessee provides a dramatic example of preservation of an embalmed body from the U. S. Civil War (Dowd, 1980). Col. Shy was killed at the Battle of Nashville on December 16, 1864, a cold, rainy, wind-blown day. The family claimed the body and had it embalmed and buried in a cast-iron coffin. Almost exactly 113 years later, Col. Shy's grave was found disturbed. The body was well preserved except for the head which had been the site of the fatal injury. The tissues of the head had not held the embalming fluid due to the massive disruption of the skull from the force of a minnie ball that must have caused instant death. Disrupted, bloody tissues also provide a medium for bacterial decomposition postmortem (Micozzi, 1986).

Embalmed bodies placed in cast-iron coffins, a rare practice during the nineteenth century, may show remarkable soft tissue preservation, as in the case of Col. Shy. Additional cast-iron coffins have been excavated by the Smithsonian Institution and the National Museum of Health and Medicine during 1988 (Park, 1988) and 1989. It is thought possible that the rusting of the cast iron coffin creates a hermetic seal and introduces antibacterial iron oxides into the environment that prevent bacterial decomposition. Further, the use of lead to line the coffin may result in lead oxides that also have bacteriacidal effects and allow preservation, especially in the presence of embalming fluids. Nonetheless, numerous soil fungi and bacteria can be identified microbiologically within these coffins.

Chapter IV

EFFECTS OF PLANTS
AND MICROBIOLOGIC ORGANISMS
ON TISSUE PRESERVATION

PLANT PRODUCTS WITH PRESERVATIVE ACTIVITY

As with many natural compounds, aromatic spices have antibacterial activity. The value of spices, as well as salts, through history has been in their ability to preserve fresh animal flesh and soft tissue, as well as their ability to disguise the foul flavor and smell of putrid meat. Spiced and salted meats could remain edible for long periods of time prior to the advent of refrigeration. In such cases, a combination of desiccation and the direct antibacterial action of these natural products preserved meat. It is adaptive for plants to manufacture chemical compounds with biological activity as protection in nature against microorganisms and arthropod plant predators. Many compounds are also known to be toxic to larger predators, including humans. Furthermore, a great diversity of different active compounds made by plants would be favored as a defense against specialized predation. The insecticidal effect of cedar oil is well known to weavers of woolens and users of cedar chests or closets. Natural plant products with antibacterial action are found in honey, cinnamon, vanilla, anise, black pepper (*Piper nigricans*), hops (Miller, 1979), and red pepper (*Capsicum sativum*). Other plant sources of products with antibacterial action include mushroom (*Agaricus bisporus*), cycad (nuts), *Laburnum senecia, Crotoleria, Heliotropium*, sassafras (safrole), and sesame seed (sesamolin). These plant products contain compounds which inhibit bacterial growth, especially when reacted under heat with amino acid and simple carbohydrates (Miller, 1979), as would be present in mummified human remains.

The antibiotic component of garlic (*Allium sativum*) consists of allicin, allylpropyl disufide, allyl disufide and other sulfur compounds (Cavallite et al., 1944). The mint plant (*Perilla frutescens*) contains flavonoids, such as quercetin pentaacetate, which have antibacterial properties (Bjeldanes and Chang, 1977). These plant products also find wide application as food condiments, in Oriental cooking (e.g. tempura), and in Japanese and Southeast Asian tobaccos. The preservative effects of tea (tannic acid) have been discussed elsewhere. Alcohol is a product of natural fermentation, or artificial steam distillation, of plant complex carbohydrate and has well known preservative effects and antibacterial activity. The bodies of Admirals Horatio Nelson and John Paul Jones (Stewart, 1907) were preserved at sea in casks of alcohol. The association between naval heroes and alcohol has not been rigorously examined.

MICROBIOLOGIC PRODUCTS WITH PRESERVATIVE ACTIVITY

Similarly, microbial competition among decay organisms for substrate leads to evolutionary development of the elaboration of substances by some micro-organisms which are toxic to others. Populations of micro-organisms inhabiting a common environment compete for nutrients and other resources. In some cases, the microbial populations excrete into the environment chemicals that are toxic or inhibitory to their competitors (Fredickson and Stephanopoulos, 1981). Thus, decay organisms may produce factors to inhibit the growth of their competitors in nature. They may have specific activity against other micro-organisms, as with penicillin and products of *Streptomyces sp.*, or may actually act as toxins to megafauna predators and scavengers, as with *Clostridium botulinum* (botulism) and *C. tetani* (tetanus). The discovery of the natural antibiotic, tetracycline, in ancient Sudanese Nubian bones, is considered to correspond to consumption of food sources contaminated with this by-product of *Streptomycetes* metabolism (Armelagos, 1980). Synthesis of antibacterial compounds by micro-organisms is shown in Table 7. Many of these compounds may also have mutagenic and carcinogenic activity (Weisburger, 1979).

Postmortem production of alcohol by anaerobic fermentation has been observed with conversion of body sugar to ethanol by bacteria. Production of alcohol commences after putrefaction has begun (Baden, 1982), and may be considered to be part of the anaerobic degradation of soft tissues which characterizes the postmortem stage of putrefaction. On a hot, humid day, putrefaction and alcohol production may occur within 6–12 hours. Elevated blood alcohol levels may thus be found postmortem, especially in diabetics with high antemortem blood sugar levels.

Table 7. Synthesis of Antibiotic Compounds by Micro-organisms

Micro-organisms	Product	Activity
Aspergillus flavus	aflatoxin A	antibacterial
	aflatoxin B	carcinogenic
A. nidulans	sterigmatocystin	antibacterial
A. versicolor		anti-cancer
Penicillium griseofulvum	griseofulvin	antimycotic
P. islandicum	luteoskyrin (polyhydroxyanthroquinone)	antibacterial
Streptomyces achromogenes	streptozotocin	antibiotic
S. antibioticus or *chrysomallus*	actinomycin D	antibiotic anti-cancer
S. hepaticus	elaiomycin	antibacterial
Streptomycetes sp.	tetracycline	antibiotic

DESTRUCTION OF PRESERVED TISSUES BY MICROBIOLOGIC ACTIVITY

Destruction of preserved mummified tissue by fungus has also been described (Mouchacca, 1977). In the mummy of Ramses V, the wrappings, the body itself and the coffin were found to harbor 80 species of fungi. Microbiological analysis revealed biodegration of the mummy of Ramses II due to foci of recent infection and a dense fungal population. Their action in retention of water was held responsible for degradation of the mummy tissues (Mouchacca, 1978). Hope (1834) provided an early description of eleven species of insects and unidentified pupae of a number of *Diptera* species found in the heads of Egyptian mummies estimated to be 3000 years old. Granville (1825) reports the experience of Hertzog who opened a mummy "in which more idols, beetles, frogs and nilometers were found than had ever been met under similar circumstances."

Chapter V

POSTMORTEM PUTREFACTION AND DECAY

Soft tissue which has not been naturally or artificially preserved is subject to the postmortem processes of putrefaction (anaerobic degradation) and decay (aerobic degradation). Whereas desiccation occurs under conditions of dryness, putrefaction takes place in the presence of moisture and moderate temperatures. No putrefaction occurs at temperature less than 4° C (the temperature of the average refrigerator). Very high moisture content may lead to saponification with conversion of soft tissues (especially fat) to adipocere or "grave wax." Great variability in decomposition rates has traditionally been reported (Baden, 1982). Some early information is available on patterns of soft tissue decay in humans (Megnin, 1887, 1894). Modern investigations of soft tissue putrefaction and decay in humans are currently in progress at the University of Tennessee under Dr. William Bass (Rodriguez and Bass, 1985). Decomposition rates of buried human cadavers are highly dependent upon depth of burial and environmental temperatures.

Decomposition of buried human cadavers occurs at a much slower rate than cadavers placed above ground. Buried cadavers are not as accessible to many carrion insects (Rodriguez and Bass, 1985), nor are they accessible to carnivores. Also, lower soil temperatures and slower decay rates are associated with deeper burials. An arid environment produces a different profile of decay in humans (Galloway et al., 1989) than that previously reported (Megnin, 1887, 1894; Motter, 1898; Rodriguez and Bass, 1983, 1985).

Under climatological conditions where both putrefaction and decay occur, soft tissue degradation proceeds from within due to the action of enteric micro-organisms, and from without by colonization with soil micro-organisms and decay organisms (Micozzi, 1986). With time, there is a succession from enteric micro-organisms to soil micro-organisms in the remains.

Phases of decay have been experimentally studied using squirrels (*Sciurus carolinensis, S. niger*), rabbits (*Sylvilagus floridanus*) and oppossum

(*Didelphis marsupialis*) (Johnson, 1975), in frogs (*Rana sp.*), toads (*Bufo sp.*), white-footed mice (*Peromyscus leucopus*), house mice (*Mus musculus*), short-tailed shrews (*Blarina brevicauda*), cotton rats (*Sigmodon hispidus*) and Eastern chipmunks (*Tamias striatus*) (Payne, 1965), and in laboratory (Wistar) rats (Micozzi, 1986).

POSTMORTEM BACTERIOLOGY AND MICROBIOLOGICAL SUCCESSION

Postmortem transformation by the action of micro-organisms has not been well studied. Bacteriologists, pathologists and physicians alike have traditionally held the view that micro-organisms rapidly multiply and disseminate throughout the human body after death (de Jongh et al., 1968). A variation on this theme is that the body tissues are rapidly colonized by bacteria as a terminal event just prior to death, a phenomenon which has been termed "agonal invasion" (Decker, 1978).

The possibility of postmortem bacterial transmigration has been pointed out by Nehring et al., (1972). Postmortem movement of intravascular fluid was noted by Morada (1968) in her study of "postmortem pulmonary edema." Movement of body fluid should be expected to facilitate migration of bacteria postmortem. Non-motile bacteria may be carried passively in fluid, and development of postmortem gas planes through tissues may also facilitate bacterial migration (Shanklin, 1972). Few studies have been performed, and little data has been collected, to test the hypothesis as to whether or not agonal invasion does occur (Carpenter and Wilkins, 1964).

One study demonstrated a positive correlation between frequency of positive bacterial cultures from heart's blood and length of postmortem interval (Carpenter and Wilkins, 1964). However, subsequent postmortem bacteriological studies have shown no increase in the frequency of positive postmortem cultures with increasing time intervals after death (de Jongh et al., 1968; Nehring et al., 1971, 1972; Dolan et al., 1971; Knapp and Kurt, 1968; O'Toole et al., 1965; Wilson et al., 1972; Minckler, 1966). The inhibitory effect of refrigeration on bacterial growth is well known, and putrefaction does not occur in refrigerated mortuaries where postmortem studies have generally been carried out.

When bacteria do appear postmortem, there have been repeated observations of discrepancies between microorganisms found during life and those present after death in a given individual (Decker, 1978). The possibility that devitalized tissues provide fertile soil for multiplication of transient bacterial inhabitants has never been proved or disproved. The relatively anoxic tissues of dying organisms provide more fertile ground for bacterial growth than do normal, healthy tissues (Koneman and Davis, 1974). Such a process must be somewhat irregular since up to 50% of postmortem cultures done under carefully controlled conditions are sterile (Minckler et al., 1966). However, still viable cultures have been obtained up to 35 days after death (Nehring et al., 1971), and a large proportion of postmortem tissues yield positive bacterial growth (Tables 8 and 9).

Table 8. Postmortem Frequency of Micro-organisms in All Normally Sterile Sites*

E. coli	18%	Staph. epiderm.	5%
Klebsiella sp.	14%	Candida	5%
Staph. aureus	8%	Enterobacer_	4%
Strep. viridans	8%	Clostridium perifringens	15%
Pseudomonus sp.	8%	Beta-hemolytic strep.	1%
Proteus sp.	8%	Diploccus pneumoniae	1%
Strep. faecalis	7%	Misc.	1%

*(Koneman and Davis, 1974)

It had been assumed that the viscera are normally sterile, except for the gastrointestinal tract. However, the human body, like that of animals, does not normally maintain a sterile internal environment (Minckler et al., 1966), and there may be normal internal bacterial microflora. Studies to date have concerned aerobic bacteria; no data are available on anaerobic bacteria. Only one study employed special methods for isolation of fungi, mycobacteria or viruses (Dolan et al., 1971). Based upon limited studies of refrigerated human remains, it appears that the length of the postmortem interval has no correlation to bacterial growth. Contamination from outside organisms, however, may readily occur postmortem. Small numbers of bacteria may be present within human tissues after death even without disease. These indigenous bacterial microflora are of uncertain origin and significance. Abundant bacterial growth is likely to be associated with infection, particularly when organisms can be identified by staining and there is histologic evidence of inflammation. Organisms seen on section may not be viable, and only microbiological studies may show evidence of viable bacteria (de Jongh, 1968).

Table 9. Relative Frequency of Micro-organisms Observed by Postmortem Time Interval*

Organisms	\	\	*Hours Postmortem*	\	\
	0–4	*4–8*	*8–12*	*12–16*	*16–20*
Anaerobic diphtheroids	•	••••	•		•
Staph. epidermis	•	••	••••	•	
Strep. viridans	•	•••	••		
Paracolon	•		•	•	•
Aerobic diptheroids	•		••	•	•
E. coli			••		•
Staph. aureus			•••		
Candida abicans		•	•		
Aerobacter aerogenes		•			
Pseudomonas aerunginosa		•	•		
Gamma streptococcus		•			
Bacteroides			•		
E. intermedia			•		
B. subtillis		•			
Enterococcus		•			

*(O'Toole et al., 1965)

CONDITIONS OF BACTERIAL AND FUNGAL GROWTH

Temperature has a direct effect on bacterial growth in both extremes of heat and cold, and in middle ranges. Freezing stops bacterial growth and preserves tissue by influencing cell division time, while boiling kills bacteria but destroys soft tissue. At temperatures below 55° F (12° C) bacterial reproduction is greatly retarded. At temperatures between 32–41° (0–5° C) bacterial multiplication stops entirely and the time required for a single bacterial cell division to occur approaches infinity. Figure 2 shows the relation between the rate of cell division of *Bacillus mycoides* and temperature (Binford, 1978b:92). Thus, 4° C provides an effective low temperature threshold below which bacterial growth is severely retarded.

At the other end of the scale is a high temperature threshold approaching the body temperature of most homeothermic animals. The susceptibility of bacteria to increased temperature, as well as decreased, has been demonstrated under controlled conditions with respect to reduced decomposition

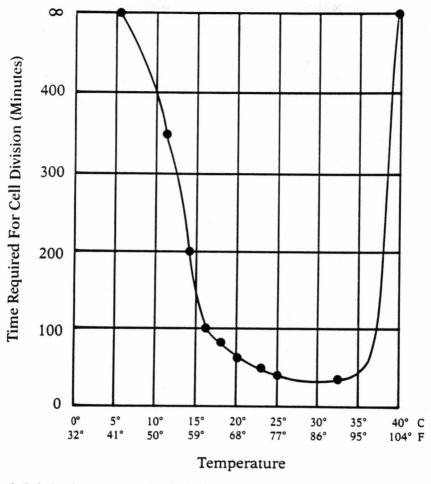

Figure 2. Relation between rate of cell division for *Bacillus mycoides* and temperature (Data from *Encyclopedia Britannica*, 1954 ed., s.v. "Bacteriology").

rates of soft tissue (Aufderheide, 1981). At high temperature, the time required for bacterial cell division approaches infinity. Thus it may be adaptive to develop a fever during infection in terms of retarding bacterial growth. However, in the temperature range immediately below this threshold, the highest rates of bacterial cell division occur. Therefore, decomposition due to bacterial action is rapid in environments characterized by temperatures between 60° and 95° F (15 and 37° C). In environments where the temperature averages between 15° and 37° C, desiccation would have to be rapid and nearly complete in order to allow even limited preservation of soft tissue. With reduction in temperature to the

5–15° C range, the degree of desiccation required for preservation would be reduced. Where temperatures are less than 5° C, the degree of desiccation would be minimal. Below 0° C, no dessication would be required (given sustained temperatures) since freezing is the most effective preservative technique (Binford, 1978:92). Prior freezing also retards bacterial growth after thawing at ambient temperature (Micozzi, 1986).

It must be considered that the temperature of decomposing soft tissue may differ widely from the ambient air or soil temperature, due to the creation of an internal microenvironment by the action of bacteria (Payne, 1965; Rodriguez and Bass, 1983, 1985). At higher temperatures, desiccation occurs more rapidly but bacterial growth is also greater. Thus the outcome of this balance at a given temperature will depend upon humidity.

Anaerobic bacteria are present both as enteric organisms in the soft tissues of the gastrointestinal tract from the mouth to the anus, and as decay organisms in the soil. They are characterized by their susceptibility to oxygen. The clostridial species are representative of anaerobic soil organisms. A lower pH as found in necrotic tissues, allows survival of anaerobic organisms at relatively higher oxygen concentrations. Furthermore, rapid death of the organism may cause acid buildup, with low pH, which destroys tissues and may facilitate growth of micro-organisms. During slow death, there is no acid buildup and soft tissues may be preserved longer.

Many fungal organisms are also ubiquitous saprophytes which thrive on dead or decaying tissue (Lehrer et al., 1980). The lower pH of necrotic or acidotic tissues provides a more appropriate milieu for the growth of these organisms as well. However, postmortem culture in patients with antemortem infection is often negative for these organisms.

DECAY SEQUENCES AND PUTREFACTION PATTERNS

While postmortem decomposition is recognized as a continual process, it is useful to divide the characteristic sequences into discrete stages for purposes of soft tissue taphonomy. Payne (1965) characterized six stages of decay in baby pigs (*Sus scrofa Linnaeus*) during summer: fresh (day 1), bloated (day 2), active decay (day 4), advanced decay (day 6), dry decay (day 8), and remains. Over ninety percent of the remains of animals exposed to arthropod activity (open to insects) were consumed within six days. Overlapping of carrion insects and soil insects occurred on the sixth day.

When animal remains were protected from insects (insect-free), decay patterns were less rapid and dramatic, with observation of only five phases: fresh (days 1–2), bloated and decomposition (days 2–3), flaccidity and dehydration (day 10), mummification (2 months), and dessication and disintegration (3 months). Fungi were observed growing in the remains during the mummification phase, and disarticulation set in by the final phase. When protected from insects, retention of antemortem size and shape persisted for long periods (Payne, 1965). It was noted that the internal temperature of the carrion itself differed widely from the ambient air or soil temperature, attributed to creation of an internal micro-climatic environment through bacterial action (Payne, 1965). Desiccation was observed to occur faster at higher ambient temperatures, but arthropod activity was also greater. Fuller (1934) observed that high temperature and very low humidity caused rapid desiccation of carrion which makes the flesh generally unavailable to insect larvae.

Four phases of decay have been observed by both Reed (1958) and Johnson (1975). Johnson (1975) described fresh, bloat, decay and dry stages. The fresh stage persisted no longer than two days. The bloat stage was characterized by the buildup of gases due to predominance of anaerobic protein decomposition by bacteria (putrefaction), and persisted from two to five days under warm conditions. In a cold environment, or when the animal was exposed to alternating freeze-thaw cycles, this phase persisted for several weeks.

During the decay phase, there was overall predominance of aerobic protein decomposition by bacteria. The decay phase occurs even without the presence of insects, due to the action of bacteria and fungi (Johnson, 1965). Fungi were also observed during the decay phase by Reed (1958) and Payne (1965). During this period, there is 90 percent weight loss to hard, dry, mummified remains. During the ensuing dry phase, all arthropods disappear but return when the remains are moistened by rain (Johnson, 1975).

Variations in the duration of the various phases or stages of putrefaction and decay have been reported (Johnson, 1975). Table 10 shows the average length of duration of the four phases by season of the year.

Extensive freezing and lack of decay organism activity during winter preclude observation of definitive decay patterns during this season. Animals that have been subjected to freezing and subsequently thaw, appear to decompose from the "outside-in" with predominantly decay due to invasion by external soil organisms, while unfrozen animals decompose from the "inside-out" with predominantly putrefaction due to enteric micro-organism dissemination (Micozzi, 1986).

Table 10. Average Duration of Decay Phases by Season

Phase	Spring (March–May)	Summer (June–August)	Fall (Sept.–Nov.)
Fresh	2 d.	1 d.	1–2 d.
Bloat	19 d.	4 d.	13 d.
Decay	23 d	13 d.	21 d.
Dry	60 d.	30 d.	52 d.

ARTHROPOD ACTIVITY AND SUCCESSION SEQUENCES

One of the earliest entomologial studies of postmortem change was conducted by Motter (1898), although case reports go back to that of Bergeret (1850).

Three categories of insects are observed on soft tissue remains (Payne, 1965; Payne and Crossley, 1966; Johnson, 1975, Early and Goff, 1986). The necrophagus insects are primary consumers of carrion, and largely include the larvae of insects that are not normally necrophagus themselves. The omnivorous insects both consume carrion from the carcass and also prey on the primary necrophagous insects. Predator and parasite insects prey only on the primary necrophagus insects, or represent secondary consumers of the primary carrion consumers. To this classification may be added a fourth (or fourth and fifth) category of insects seeking shelter (non-carrion insects) and chance (accidental) inhabitants of carrion (Goff, Omori, Gunatilake, 1988).

Payne (1965) and Johnson (1975) have observed a succession sequence by arthropod order predominance with respect to decay and putrefaction phases, as shown in Table 11.

Insect activity is at a maximum during the decay phase. The abundance and specificity of organisms for a given decay stage is indicated in Table 12. The presence of non-carrion insects, such as ants, may slow decomposition rates because they remove the fly larvae that are feeding on carrion (Rodriguez and Bass, 1983).

A total of 522 species representing 3 phyla, 9 classes, 31 orders, 151 families and 359 genera were collected from decomposing pigs (Payne, 1965). The four orders of anthropods shown in the table represented 78–90 percent of the carrion micro-fauna. Two families of Coleoptera (Histeridae, Staphylinidae) and three families of Diptera (Sarcophagidae,

Table 11. Arthropod Succession Sequences

Decay Phase	Diptera	Coleoptera	Hymenoptera	Arandeida
	Arthropod Order (Relative Frequency)			
Fresh	•••	•		
Bloat	••	••	•	
Decay	•	•••	•••	•
Dry			•	

Calliphoridae and Muscidae) alone accounted for one-fourth of the micro-fauna.

There were variations in anthropod activity by time of night and day during diurnal cycle. Variations in insect activity have also been reported by season (Johnson, 1975). Urban insect populations have also been found to vary by geographic region within the United States, including Arizona, Kansas, Michigan, New York and West Virginia (Schoof et al., 1956).

Climatological influences on insect activity have also been observed. Calliphorid flies and larvae are generally inactive on cool, cloudy days and completely outmigrate during wet weather (Graham-Smith, 1916; Payne, 1965). The larvae of the screw-worm and sheep blow-fly are extremely sensitive to moisture (Brannon, 1934). In contrasting tropical habitats, variations in carrion insect activity are also observed (Cornaby, 1974; Jiron and Cartin, 1981).

Similar insect populations are observed in flowers, feces, garbage,

Table 12. Stage-Specificity of Insect Species

Phase	Total Number of Species	Percentage of these species attracted (in abundance) to another decay phase		
		Number and percentage of insect species attracted to various stages of decay		
Fresh	17	—	94%	76–94%	0
Bloated	48	33%	—	90–100%	2%
Decay	426	3–6%	10–19%	—	13–38%
Dry	211	0	›1%	16–76%	—
		Fresh	Bloat	Decay	Dry

decaying fruits and fungi. Insect activity is at a maximum during the aerobic decay phase of decomposition and represents decay from without. During earlier phases of anaerobic putrefaction, internal decay processes predominate. Insect activity may also result in destruction of bone as well as soft tissue (Brothwell, 1963).

A series of ongoing studies conducted at the University of Tennessee on decaying human cadavers has shed additional light on the relevance of insect activity to postmortem processes (Rodriguez and Bass, 1983). These studies indicate that there is a direct correlation between the rate of decay and the succession of insect families and species found in association with a human cadaver which is comparable to the animal experimental observations.

Aquatic insects are found in association with human and animal remains submerged in water. Certain aquatic animals such as chironomid midges (Diptera, Chironomidae) and caddisflies (Trichoptera) may colonize immersed remains (Hawley et al., 1989; Haskell, et al., 1989). The utilization of aquatic insects in determining postmortem interval has not been exploited in the past, however.

CURATORIAL LOSSES OF SOFT TISSUE

Soft tissues may be preserved by artificial or natural means, yet be subject to skeletonization on the basis of curatorial practices. Loss of soft tissue may occur in transfer of remains from the systemic to archaeologic contexts; or within the archaeologic context, through decay and other postmortem modification. Loss of soft tissue due to curatorial practices may also occur in transfer of remains from archaeologic back into systemic context. Adelson (1974:137) had recommended to forensic pathologists that they clean skeletal remains of soft tissues prior to forwarding to forensic anthropologists. Forensic anthropologists are now discovering the utility of soft tissue for identification and interpretation of human remains (Saul and Micozzi, 1988, 1989). The intentional unwrapping and burning of Egyptian mummies has been discussed in Chapter III, and unintentional curatorial losses of soft tissue are only too obvious with the Royal Mummies kept in Cairo.

Intentional losses of soft tissue have also occurred through curatorial practices. Aleutian mummies, discovered in a volcanic cave on Kagamil Island in 1938, by Hrdlicka, were skeletonized for inclusion in the Smithsonian Institution Osteological Collection. Methods for the preparation of skeletal materials from preserved soft tissues have long been employed (Skinner, 1926). Over 3000 skeletons were prepared from soft tissues in the Hamann-Todd Collection at Case Western Reserve University (Cobb, 1959). The boiling of human and animal bones has also been practiced for removal of soft tissues.

In ancient China, the clavicles and scapulae of domesticated sheep and goats were boiled for preparation of "oracle bones" and inscribed with ancient Chinese script. The use of very large bronze cauldrons dating to the period has remained unexplained by Chinese art historians. Their use in preparation of oracle bones has been suggested by the author.

In terms of curatorial preservation of the skeleton, all too often in the course of nineteenth century excavation, only the skull was kept for permanent preservation by archaeologists, with the post-cranial skeleton discarded or reburied as having little or no anthropological value (Brothwell, 1967).

Chapter VI

TRANSFORMATION OF
THE SKELETON AND BONE

SKELETONIZATION AND DISARTICULATION SEQUENCES

A human body buried in the ground takes an average of seven years to skeletonize completely in the experience of forensic pathologists (Baden, 1982). Organic remains on the surface, exposed to decay organisms and scavengers, skeletonize more rapidly (Payne, 1965; Johnson, 1975). Decomposition of soft tissue occurs from the top (head) downward, similar to the progression of rigor mortis as an immediate postmortem process. Insect activity begins with destruction of mucous membranes and openings and cavities in the body. A shallow depth of burial facilitates more rapid decomposition due to plant and animal activity. Rodriguez and Bass (1985) have shown that a burial at two feet depth requires six months to skeletonize, while a burial at (the traditional) six feet requires two years. Underground, the body bloats, pushes up soil and causes subsequent deflation to the soil with decay.

Once soft tissue has been removed, the process of skeletal disarticulation begins rapidly. Patterns of disarticulation may be based upon natural intrinsic decay processes, or related to the actions of humans or other predators and scavengers (Binford, 1981; Crader, 1974). Insect larvae may actually scatter and remove bones, even in situations where no scavenger or carnivore activity is possible. Mechanical determinants of intrinsic disarticulation sequences are based upon principles of syndesmology, which determine the relative strength, resistance and integrity of joints in the body. Because the nature of the articulations and the character of the organic materials involved vary with the mechanical type of joint, it is reasonable to assume that these various sites may be differentially effected by decay and disarticulation processes.

Joints, or articulations, can be relatively immovable with sutural ligaments, as in the skull. Articulations can also be slightly movable as with fibrocartilage in the vertebrae and interpubic joints. Finally, joints can be freely movable, as with hyaline cartilage and synovial capsules, in the standard articulations of long bones. Embryologically, the mesodermal middle layer of tissue develops into three histological types of cartilages and connective tissues as shown in Table 13. A synarthrosis (e.g., skull) may be a suture (e.g. dentata, serrata, limbosa), schindylesis, gomphosis (as with teeth) or synchondrosis. An amphiarthrosis (e.g., vertebrae) may be a symphysis (e.g., pubis) or a syndesmosis (e.g., sacroiliac) held by an intraosseous ligament, as with the inferior tibial-fibular ligament. A diarthrosis has articular cartilage and can be uniaxial, as with a ginglymus (transverse) joint, or trochoid or pivot-joint (longitudinal, e.g., radio-ulnar).

A biaxial diarthrosis can be condyloid (e.g., wrist) or saddle joint (e.g., thumb). A poly-axial diarthrosis, or enarthrosis, is a ball-and-socket joint (e.g., hip, shoulder). An arthroidial diarthrosis is a gliding joint, as in the vertebral facets, carpals, and tarsals. The mandible is somewhat special, considered to be a ginglymo-arthroidial joint. Patterns of disarticulation may differ involving these various morphologic joint types.

Table 13. Types and Functions of Joints

Tissue Type	Joint Type	Function	Example
Fibrous tissue	Synarthroidial	Immovable	Skull bones
Partly cartilaginous	Amphiarthroidial	Slightly moveable	Sacroiliac
Synovium	Diarthroidial	Free movement	Knee, hip

Natural patterns of decay and disarticulation provide a data base upon which the activities of humans (in the form of dismemberment) and other predators and scavengers, are superimposed. However, few definitive studies of natural skeletal disarticulation have been done (Binford, 1981: ch. 3). Although sequences of natural dismemberment have been proposed by Hill (1977, 1979, 1980), these studies are ambiguous in that the activity of decay organisms and intrinsic chemical processes is not distinguished from that of predator-scavenger carnivores.

Whether through dismemberment, carnivore activity, or natural weathering, the material strength of articulations and the amount and nature of connective tissue separating bones in joints strongly influence disarticulation patterns. Various biological and physical agents such as freezing-thawing (Micozzi, 1986), may accelerate the process of disarticulation, but do not alter its sequence (Gifford, 1981). Disarticulation by passive agents, such as micro-organisms and invertebrate activity, and even active agents, such as vertebrate carnivores, are based upon the intrinsic properties of bones and joints. However, the use of tools by humans for dismemberment, and other patterns produced by human behavior may circumvent those mandated by natural physical properties. Dismemberment practices by various ethnic groups, including the Akamba, Masai, Kalinjmo, Navajo, !Kung and Nunamiut, have been described (Binford, 1981:92).

Disarticulation of the first and second cervical vertebrae is observed early in the sequence of disarticulation in both animals (Micozzi, 1986) and humans (Rodriguez and Bass, 1985). The mandible and skull generally have the first opportunity to become disarticulated from the remainder of the skeleton (Table 14). As with the observed decomposition of soft tissue (Rodriguez and Bass, 1985) natural skeletal disarticulation sequences generally proceed from the top (mandible and skull) downward, and centrally (vertebrae) to peripherally (limbs). Thus, the mandible and skull have the first opportunity to become mechanically separated from the remainder of the body, and these most visible and identifiable skeletal elements are often not found in association with the less-identifiable post-cranial remains. This pattern is consistent with the observations on mammalian skeletal remains in archaeologic context where mandibles and skulls are usually found in isolation (Dodson, 1973; Boaz and Behrensmeyer, 1976; Brain, 1981; Hill, 1979). In humans, Ubelaker (1974:66) suggests that the lower leg bone articulation could be maintained as long as eight months, even allowing for the winter, in mid-Atlantic Indians placed in death houses or on scaffolds, and protected from many, though not all, scavengers.

RANGE AND RELATIONS OF
RELEVANT TAPHONOMIC FACTORS

Skeletonized remains may be acted upon by a number of biological agents, including carnivores (humans and other predators and scavengers), micro-organisms and plants. Postmortem manipulation of human remains by other humans may occur with bones as well as with soft tissues (Cybulski, 1978). Patterned destruction of human bones at one site in the southwestern United States revealed evidence of dismemberment, mutilation and possible roasting of human bones postmortem (Flinn et al., 1976). The issue of human cannibalism is complex and controversial, ranging from arguments about *Homo erectus* at Choukoutien (Peking man) to present day tribes on the Andaman Islands. Humans may also modify animal bones postmortem in very specific patterns, as with "oracle bones" in ancient China (see Chap. V).

Table 14. Vertebrate Disarticulation Sequences in the Rat
with and without Freezing Postmortem

	Time Interval (days)	
Disarticulation Order	*Fresh*	*Frozen*
Tempero-mandibular	2–4	2–4
Atlanto-occipital	4–6	2–4
Cervical vertebrae	4–6	2–4
Symphysis pubis	4–6	2–4
Lumbar vertebrae	4–6	4–6
Sterno-costal	4–6	4–6
Costo-vertebral	› 6	4–6
Lumbo-sacral	› 6	4–6
Sacro-iliac	› 6	4–6
Pelvic-hip	› 6	4–6
Knee	› 6	2–6
Upper extremity	› 6	› 6
Lower extremity	› 6	› 6

In archaeologic context, histological and ultrastructural features of postmortem bone destruction by micro-organisms has been ascribed to solubilization and decalcification of bone matrix (Marchiafava et al., 1974). Plant roots may produce etching of bone surfaces ("arte mobiliar") by the action of acids found in compact root masses (Binford, 1981:ch. 3). The death of an animal only rarely leads to preservation of bones on site, and articulated bones are rarely observed (Binford, 1978:64).

Postmortem modification of animal bones as it relates to human activity is determined by hunting patterns, butchery techniques, meat (and bone) distribution and cooking and culinary practices. Natural factors of bone modification come into primary play at the point at which bones are "discarded" by the human groups. This discard activity may occur into domestic systemic context, e.g., Nunamiut Eskimo dogyards (Binford,

1978), natural systemic context with wild carnivores, or directly into archaeologic context as mixed bulk disposal into middens. The creation of zones of discard has been discussed by Binford (1978).

Characteristics of carnivore behavior differ between human and animal activity. Patterns of bone breakage, degree of destruction and "ravaging" by carnivores may be distinguished from the disposition and character of tracings made on bones by humans due to skinning, butchering and meat processing procedures. The implementation of experimental studies and development of analytical procedures are useful in determining breakage patterns, survivorship of anatomic elements and "cut marks" characteristic of butchery practices.

Binford and Bertram (1977, 1978, 1981) investigated Alaskan Eskimo butchery and processing techniques, and wild wolf kills and lairs, to determine distinctive "diagnostic" patterns for these activities in bone. Ethno-archaeologic studies have been carried out in Africa by Yellen (1977), Gifford (1981) and Crader (1974). Specific studies of taphonomic principles have been attempted by Behrensmeyer (1975), Hill (1975), and Shipman (1975). Carnivore accumulations (e.g. hyena dens) have been explored by Sutcliffe (1970), and Klein (1980).

Selective preservation of specific anatomic elements has been observed due to selective human activity, such as butchering (Clark, 1960; Howell, 1961) and tool-making (Dart, 1957); weathering (Isaac, 1967) and carnivore predation and scavenging activity (Brain, 1967; Sutcliffe, 1970).

Finally, poor preservation of bone due to natural conditions is likely with sites located in areas undergoing deflation or erosion, and subject to extremes of wet and dry (Binford, 1981:ch. 2; Wood and Johnson, 1978). Preservation is more likely at sites on the margins of bodies of water, river deltas, and in caves and rockshelters (Gifford, 1981).

The intrinsic properties of bone, such as size and durability, play an important role in their disposition, from size-based butchery and transport decisions, to the effects of bone weathering and soil disturbance processes. Scavenger activity, geologic processes, and other taphonomic factors may enter the postmortem history at multiple and varied times and interfaces. Soil transformations affect bone like any other archaeologic material. Finally, excavation techniques and curatorial practices directly affect "survivability" and "recognizability" and lead either to preservation of remains or to information losses.

DIFFERENTIAL SURVIVABILITY
OF BONE—NATURAL PROCESSES

The differential survival probability of anatomic parts is determined by the attritional processes which modify skeletal assemblages, as discussed by Binford and Bertram (1977). However, what may be called survivability is also influenced by the individual characteristics and attributes of bone itself. For instance, survivability has been directly related to the density of a bone. If taphonomy represents a truly dynamic interaction between bone and the archaeologic matrix, as defined by Binford (1981), a prima facie discussion of the nature of bone itself is of direct relevance.

Bone is not a uniform substance. It may be characterized into four types by gross morphology, three types by gross structure, and two types by microscopic architecture.

Table 15. Classification of Human Bones

Long bones (cortical)	Flat bones (membranous)	Short bones	Irregular
mandible	frontal	carpals	vertebrae (cervical,
clavicle	parietals	metacarpals	thoracic, lumbar,
humerus	occipital	tarsals	coccyx)
radius	temporal (squamous)	metatarsals	temporal (petrous)
ulna	sternum (manubrium,	phalanges	sphenoid
femur	gladiolus, xyphoid)		maxilla
tibia	scapula		nasal
fibula	sacrum		zygomatic
	ilium		ethmoid
	ischium		lacrimal
	pubis		palate
	ribs		vomer
			inferior nasal concha
			malleus, incus, stapes
			hyoid
			patella

The four gross morphologic types of bone are long, short, flat and irregular (Table 15). The long bones include the humerus, radius, ulna, femur, tibia and fibula. The short bones appear in the hands and feet. Matacarpals and metatarsals have the internal structure of long bones, and the carpals and tarsals are somewhat irregular, leaving the phalanges as true short bones. The flat bones include the crania, ribs, sternum, scapulae and pelvis. The irregular bones are represented by the vertebrae and certain bones of the face and skull. The mandible is somewhat exceptional, composed of dense cortical bone.

There are two types of bone architecture. The tissue within an individual skeletal element may consist of compact bone, or cancellous (spongy) bone. Compact bone is a dense mass of lamellar bone comprising the full thickness of a bone wall or cortex, as in the shaft of a long bone. Cancellous bone is a porous network of branching and anastomosing trabecular bone, as found in articular ends, centrum of the vertebrae and centers of other bones.

The three topographic regions of tissue structure within a bone are compact cortical bone in the mid-portion of long bone shafts, the medullary cavity containing marrow in the center of long bones and trabecular bone in the articular ends.

The relative proportions and distribution of dense cortical bone to spongy cancellous bone influence the differential survival and susceptibility to modification of certain bones over others, and of certain parts of a given bone over other parts, by all attritional agents of postmortem change.

In addition, certain antemortem pathological condition of bone affect the density and differential survival of skeletal elements. Table 16 shows pathologic influences on bone density.

Another type of microscopic bone architecture is woven bone, which occurs as an early response to injury, and is less dense than lamellar bone. It may occur in pathologic states where there is a stimulus for rapid bone growth, as in fracture repair or bone tumors (e.g., osteosarcoma).

Some conditions may increase the absolute amount of tissue in a bone, while decreasing the cortical/trabecular bone ratio, as in fibrous dysplasia. Soft tissue may also become calcified in various pathologic conditions and act as bone. Muscle may become calcified in myositis ossificans and the respiratory tract may become bone in tracheopathia osteoplastica. Leiomyomata (uterine fibroid tumors) and even occluded blood vessels may also become calcified and undergo metaplasia to bone. Thus, patterns of pathology as related to density will lead to differential survival of bone and even calcified soft tissue in the archaeologic record.

The primary non-pathologic determinants of bone survivability related to density (mass: volume) are age, species, size and nutritional status.

Age has a biphasic relationship to bone density within a species. Young animals have relatively low bone density. As adult age and sexual

Table 16. Pathologic Influences on Bone Density

Increased Density:	Decreased Density:
osteomalacia (sometimes)	osteopenia
healed fracture	healing fracture
acromegaly	early rheumatoid arthritis
metatastic tumor (osteoblastic)	metastatic tumor (osteolytic)
ankylosing spondylitis	osteoporosis
tertiary and endemic syphilis	osteogenesis imperfecta
osteoarthritis (DJD)	porotic hyperostosis
osteophytosis	leprosy
osteochondroma	pyogenic osteomyelitis
enchondroma	skeletal tuberculosis
osteoid osteoma	solitary bone cyst
fibrous dysplasia	hemangioma
myositis ossificans	osteoclastoma
	histicytosis
	multiple myeloma

maturation are reached, there are growth and developmental increases in bone density. The process has been described as non-allometric densification of bone with age (Binford and Bertram, 1977). Later, with old age, hormonal changes, especially in females, cause decreased bone density or osteoporosis. Binford (1978) states that young animals are more subject to seasonal variations and nutritional deficiencies with differential bone densification. This phenomenon has been observed in animals and humans as "Harris lines." In addition to its relationship to nutritional density of bone, seasonality has an independent effect on bone density. That is, the time of year an animal dies influences bone density. However, patterns of decay are strongly influenced by season and will exercise proximal effects at the time of death which may mask the primary effects of bone density itself through time.

The size of an individual bone also relates to its density. Binford and Bertram (1977) incorrectly invoke scaling principles to demonstrate that larger bones have a greater surface area to volume ratio. The reverse is actually true; namely, that larger bones have smaller surface area to volume ratios, since the volume increases as the cube of the diameter, while the area increases as the square of the diameter, with increasing bone size (unidimensional radius, diameter or length). It is true that bones from larger animals must be stronger (more dense) in life, since they must support relatively heavier animals. Since weight is a function of volume, the mass of the animal increases as the cube of unidimensional increases in height, length or width. Since the time of Galileo it has been known that bone thickness must increase relatively more than bone length as body size increases in order to provide sufficient support for the added mass of the animal. Thus, skeletal mass occupies a greater fraction of body mass in larger animals, as determined from cleaned and dried museum skeletal specimens (Calder, 1984). It is also worthy of note, for example, that the metatarsal bone of a rabbit is 40 percent stronger when recovered with skin intact than when tested as dry bone (Currey 1968). Skin may properly be considered as contributing to the survival of the bone under certain circumstances.

Furthermore, Binford's age effect may be confounded by his size effect, in that younger animals of a species have less survivable bones because they are less dense, while they may have more survivable bones because they are smaller. The independent relationship of bone density to size, not just density with age, and age with size, is relevant here.

However, Binford and Bertram (1977) report higher attrition rates for analogous parts from larger animals. They explain that large animals have increased surface area of articular ends of weight-bearing joints as a function of increased body weight. The greater surface area of articular ends results in their differential destruction. By the same token, the shafts of long bones must also be stronger, denser and, therefore, more survivable. Thus, while articular ends may not survive, bone shafts will survive in larger animals. However, the midshaft of a bone is less recognizable than its characteristic articular ends, and the archaelogic visibility and survivability of a large bone may be lower in this sense.

This phenomenon points out that differential recognizability, or "archaeologic visibility," is a corollary to differential survivability. The ability of a bone to survive is really the archaeologic ability to recognize it in a closed system. A further index of differential survivability of parts of individual bones would relate to their recognizability as well. For example, articular ends are more distinctive of organic material (1) as bone, (2) which bone, and (3) which species. While these considerations relate to the strength of individual bones by porosity or density, the strength of attritional agents which act upon bone must also be taken into account. Postmortem modifications to dry bone may be caused by a number of physical agents. The primary factor is chemical erosion, dependent upon temperature, soil type and acidity, moisture, method of burial and the structural-chemical status of bone at death (Ubelaker, 1989). Mechanical erosion develops over long periods of time from small movements of bone against hard surfaces, such as a floor or coffin ("coffin wear"). Unburied bones exposed to sun for prolonged periods exhibit bleaching and brittleness. Salt water may also cause bleaching, as well as other indicators such as algal deposits and barnacles.

DIFFERENTIAL SURVIVABILITY OF BONE—CULTURAL PROCESSES

We must go back one step to the process of differential deposition of bone into the archaeologic matrix, prior to its becoming a part of that matrix, in order to fully understand survivability. Differential use of anatomic parts in humans and animals in the systemic context is relevant to differential deposition (Binford, 1978).

Criteria for preferential selection of animals and animal parts for use by humans are conditioned by a number of variables, including seasonality, nutritional and ethnographic factors. For example, the Navajo select sheep for butchery based upon factors of fatness, age and fertility. Economic considerations may also be distinguished from animal behavior and social factors. For example, while an uncastrated male may be larger (more meat), his behavior may be disruptive to the overall herd and militate against optimal management (Chaplin 1969).

Modification of bone may be related to conditioned consumption, deletion or disposal. During consumption, long bones may be broken in half for extraction of marrow, with the articular ends left intact. Deletion occurs when animal feet are left on the hide, and do not accompany the remainder of the skeleton through subsequent transformation. Disposal of bones to dogs, or in mixed bulk, further conditions what comes out of systemic contexts. Seasonality also influences what goes into disposal systems, as with caribou remains fed to Eskimo dogs (Binford, 1978).

Ethnographic influences on bone modification have been studied by Binford (1978) at a Navajo summer site and at Nunamiut Eskimo dogyards. Brain (1969) examined a Hottentot goat sample, and Dart (1957) looked at bones surviving from Makapansgat fauna. Much of ethnographic data is so specific as to have limited utility for general prediction (Binford and Bertram, 1977).

For example, Yellen (1977) attributed greater survival of smaller animal bones among the !Kung to human behavior patterns and "trampling," as discussed in Chapter VII under "Actions of Noncarnivores." There also may be secondary use of animal parts, not primarily related to consumption and disposal. For example, antlers of caribou may be used by Eskimos to indicate meat caches, since they remain visible on the ground surface after subsequent deposits of snow. Animal products may also be used as components of temporary facilities for these purposes.

Ceremonial alteration of human bones postmortem is infrequent but widespread. Skulls may be mounted on wood shafts (Vignati, 1930), hung in houses, painted (Hrdlicka, 1905), and employed as containers (Ubelaker, 1989). Artistically decorated human skulls have been found from ancient Jericho (circa 7000 B.C.) to contemporary tribes on the Sepik River in New Guineau.

BEHAVIOR AND EFFECTS OF CARNIVORES ON BONES

Much patterned destruction and processing of human and animal bones postmortem may occur through the action of predators and scavengers. In systemic regional biospheres, predators may remove up to 10 percent of the total prey biomass annually (Schaller, 1972 in Binford, 1981:ch. 2).

The types and amounts of bone material which may be expected to enter into the archaeologic record as a result of predation vary by geographic region, climate and habitat. Environmental situations may either facilitate or disfavor accumulation of human and animal remains. The predominant actions of predators, and species of predators present, also vary by region. Table 17 on regional bone accumulation is adapted from data in Binford (1981:ch. 2), modified to hold constant the number of significant figures in each estimate within each region.

A predator is a carnivore (including humans) that has first access to prey "on the hoof." Scavengers modify remains at a point when soft tissues are partially or completely absent and the skeleton partially or completely disarticulated. Ecologic studies have recently shown that animals thought primarily to be scavengers, such as hyenas, may also act as predators, and vice versa (such as lions). Certain species-specific behaviors have also been observed for scavengers. Many of the so-called scavengers may also act as primary predators (Kruuk, 1972). Porcupines

Table 17. Archaeologic Bone Accumulation by Region

Habitat	Game Sample	Secondary Biomass (kg/km²)	Prey Biomass (kg/km²)	Bone Accumulation
Northern, Polar, Arctic*	Caribous			
Tundra		79	7.1	Minor
Boreal Forest		2.0	0.2	Minor
Temperate**	Ungulates			
Mixed broadleaf forest		450	40.5	Minor
Prairie grassland		3,450	310	Substantial
Tropical*	Ungulates, Primates			
Acacia savanna		15,760	1,418	Major
Rain forest		5.0	0.5	Minor

*McCullough, 1970
**Bourliere, 1963, 1966

have been observed to carry individual bones for significant distances away from the site of original deposition (Alexander, 1956, Thomas, 1971). Hyenas act as scavengers as well as predators (Hughes, 1954) and may crush, gnaw, digest and collect bones (Sutcliffe, 1970). The Masai of East Africa expose the bodies of their deceased tribesmen to the effects of scavenging by hyenas. The activity of the leopard as a scavenger has also been described (Simons, 1966, Brain, 1968 in Crader, 1974). Patterns of scavenger activity by vultures has been described in Rhodesia (Zimbabwe) (Attwell, 1963) and in West Africa (Kruuk, 1972). The behavior of owls as bone collectors has been characterized by Brain (1981). The predominance of activities of various scavengers is determined by their individual ecological niches and natural habitat distributions which may be determined by zoological studies.

A sequence of scavenger activity was observed in Zambia on remains of a buffalo (*Syncerus caffer*) after butchering by humans (Crader, 1974). Since large animals cannot be carried back to camp in one piece, they are characteristically butchered on site. In this case, the ribs, pelvis, sacrum, and lumbar and caudal vertebrae were taken to camp; the remainder of the skeleton was left at the kill site. On the first day, hyena activity was observed, with all bones removed from the immediate kill site. An area of 120 square meters around the site contained only the skull, minus mandible (brain not extracted), both scapulae and two vertebral spines. On day two, vultures were observed, as well as the African wild cat (*Felis*

Lybica), generally considered a primary predator. All remaining bone had been disturbed from the previous day. On day three, the remaining bone was observed to be not further disturbed. Small beetles and other insects were present in bone tissues, and marked desiccation from sun exposure was noted. On day four, there was no evidence of new disturbance.

The activity of hyenas as scavengers has been well demonstrated. When subject to intensive scavenging by hyenas, a yearling wildebeest was seen to disappear in 13 minutes, a gazelle fawn in only 2 minutes, and a female zebra and her two-year foal in 36 minutes and 24 minutes, respectively (Kruuk, 1972). In general, if any bone is remaining at the kill site following standard scavenging activity, it usually consists of the skull, vertebrae, ribs, pelvis and articular ends of large leg bones (Crader, 1974).

The degree of skeletal articulation and association with meat may bias the behavior of carnivores away from primary density patterns (Binford and Bertram, 1977). Behrensmeyer (1973) observed differential preservation of proximal and distal ends of various limb elements, attributed to carnivore activity. Dodson (1973) has determined disarticulation sequences resulting from carnivore activity. The degree to which bones have been processed by carnivores determines the character of the surviving skeletal remains. The characteristic skeletal assemblage patterns produced by carnivore activity include several regular features in surviving long bone parts (Binford, 1981: 171). Four morphologies of bone breakage attributed to carnivore activity are (1) articular ends, (2) end plus shank, (3) end plus shaft, and (4) cylinder.

MORPHOLOGIC MODIFICATIONS OF BONES BY CARNIVORES

Bones are regularly and extensively processed and manipulated by animals (other than man), and the actions of carnivores may affect the survival and topography of bones in the archaeologic record. Carnivores follow both economic strategies of moving consumers to goods, and goods to consumers. Carnivores may also alter the morphology of bone surviving in the archaeologic record.

The characteristic patterns of bone modification have been determined with animals considered strictly as mechanical agents of modification, primarily by the use of teeth (Binford, 1981: ch. 3), the hardest organic substance in mammals. The teeth of carnivores may be considered as "denticulated vises" for these purposes.

The morphological traits resulting in modified bone through the action of predators and scavengers have been experimentally determined (Binford, 1981: ch. 3). Tooth marks may be represented as punctures, with crenulated edges, pits, scores and furrows.

Table 18 shows typical modified bone appearance and the corresponding carnivore or human activity that may produce it, using some terms cited by Binford (1981:ch. 3) and others extrapolated from his gross descriptions.

Table 18. Patterns of Carnivore Modification in Bone

| Morphologic Trait | Behavior | |
	Animal Activity	Human Technology
(1) Channelization "step fractures"	"direct" bite down	
(2) "Chipped back"	"mashing off" microchips	"microdenticulate" lithic technology
(3) Mashed edges	"vise-down"	"use wear"
(4) Longitudinal split splinters with chipped edges		worked points, edges

These morphological traits are likely to involve different bones to varying extents. The typical findings of carnivore activity on specific bones are shown in Table 19.

The internal structure of the bone determines the character of the fracture or other modification. General trends include greater proximal than distal destruction (esp. humerus), and greater destruction of articular ends with preservation of the mid-shaft. Longitudinally split fragments with denticulated ends, collapsed cylinders with chipped back ends and spiral fractures are characteristic of bone modification by carnivores.

Breaks in at least one ramus of the mandible across the diastemeric position are frequent due to the actions of carnivores in producing a "wishbone" effect. Carnivores may also consume some boney anatomic parts, including the entire tail with caudal vertebrae (Hill, 1976). Absence of the caudal vertebrae has also been ascribed to human activity (Dart, 1957).

The major differential in identifying and determining agents of bone modification is between the butchering activities of humans and the predatory and scavenging activities of carnivores. Both activities may be present at the same site, as observed in Zambia (Crader, 1974). Specific

Table 19. Bone-Specific Modifications by Carnivores

Bone	Traits
Skull	channeling, crenulation skull discs or bowls depressed fractures
Mandible	punctures "wear edges"
Vertebrae	gnawing spines and processes
Ribs	"mashed back" gnawing of distal ends
Pelvis	preferential bone destruction; fractures, punctures, mashing, scarring, pitting, crenulation
Scapula	crenulation
Humerus	destruction of proximal portion
Radius-ulna	durable, gnawing; chipping back, polishing
Metacarpals and Metatarsals	"all or none" phenomenon present intact or completely absent
Femur	neck and trochanter destroyed
Tibia-Fibula	like radius and ulna (above)

traits may help distinguished butchery by humans from consumption by carnivores. A comparison of superficial taphonomic traits between human and animals activity is shown in Table 20.

Binford (1981:ch. 3) has characterized species-specific patterns produced by large carnivores. Bones at wolf skill sites show primary evidence of eating with some furrowing and relatively common puncture marks with some crenulated edges; pitting and scoring are less common. Bones in Eskimo dogyards show evidence of gnawing, by contrast, with extensive pitting and scoring and more extensive furrowing. Large mammals, such as dogs, coyotes and wolves, tend to gnaw on the ends of long bones, destroying the articular surfaces and epiphyses, while bears tend to break the diaphyses of long bones and may perforate bone with their canines (Murad and Boddy, 1987). Small animals, such as rodents and porcupines, show patterns of nibbling and gnawing (Thomas, 1971; Krogman and Iscan, 1985:37). The behavior of predators and scavengers may vary under different conditions, such as starvation. Bone assemblages may also vary by animal usage area (Binford, 1981:58). The patterns of carnivore activity associated with canids were recently observed among 37 partially to fully skeletonized human remains recovered from outdoor locations in the Seattle/King County area of Washington State between 1979 and 1987 (Haglund, Reay, Swindler, 1988, 1989), and among 30 Oneota skeletons from a west-central Illinois cemetery dated circa A.D. 1300 (Miller and Smith, 1989).

Table 20. Comparison of Taphonomic Traits Between Human and Animal Activity on Bone

	Carnivore Teeth Marks		Distinguishable Patterns of Human Technology
Animal Activity	*Primary*	*Secondary*	
Eating soft, cancellous bone	puncture	crenulated edges, furrowing	butchering-choppers "muscle stripping"
Gnawing hard, cortical bone	pitting		"compressor" tools pressure flakes
	scoring	linear scar	"cut marks"
Turning bone against teeth	follows bone contours (transverse to long axis) midshaft		pulling blade along bone follows long axis (perpendicular or angular to bone contours) articular ends 1) skinning 2) disarticulation

Distinctive alterations by carnivores of the spatial, morphologic and superficial features of bone may predominate in some regions, and within some sites, due to species present, specific behavior within species, and nutritional conditions.

Chapter VII

TRANSPORTATION AND DEPOSITION OF THE SKELETON AND BONE

ACTIONS OF NONCARNIVORES ON BONES

Breakage of bone may also occur unrelated to primary consumption by trampling and other forms of manipulation by large mammals (Binford, 1981: ch. 3). Increasing trampling by large animals is likely to occur along the margins of large bodies of water (Gifford, 1978), which is just where bones are otherwise more likely to be preserved in the archaeologic record due to environmental conditions. Some of the largest mammals may have a profound effect on deposition of bone in soil through deflation and solution. Many of the topographic depressions on the high and central plains of North America originate from the wallowing activities of American bison (Wood and Johnson, 1978).

Gifford (1978:82) has established several testable hypotheses regarding the effects of trampling on bone assemblages, recognizing the distinction between primary and secondary refuse at a site: (1) given a permeable substrate, normal occupation activities on a site ("trampling") generate a subsurface zone of like-sized items, definable within a given range of maximum dimensions, and a surface zone composed of all items of large maximum dimensions; (2) the amount of subsurface migration of fragments due to trampling depends directly upon the permeability of the substrate and the amount of trampling activity; (3) the greater the median grain size of the subsurface, the larger the median maximum dimensions of elements migrating subsurface; (4) elements below 3 cm maximum diameter are likely to become primary refuse, while larger elements are likely to become secondary refuse; (5) elements likely to be primary refuse are also those elements likely to migrate subsurface due to trampling; and (6) a subsurface trampling zone contains a relatively higher proportion of primary refuse than does the surface zone of a site.

In ethnoarchaeologic research on the !Kung bushmen, Yellen (1977) observed that the bones remaining on the surface after trampling tended to be those of larger animals, especially the distinctive articular ends.

65

Resulting subsurface large animal remains were largely smaller, non-identifiable fragments. However, nearly all identifiable bone not trampled into the substrate during occupation was rapidly consumed by animals. Any marrow bearing bone was processed by carnivores. Non-carnivores (e.g., bovids) consumed remaining bone to obtain minerals. Thus, the identifiable fragments of small animals were trampled under and protected, while the identifiable fragments of larger animals stayed on the surface and were consumed. The selective destruction of large animal bones skewed the large species representation in the recoverable sample by as much as 50 percent. While carnivores consume bone for bone marrow protein, non-carnivores may also consume bone for the bone matrix minerals. Primary consumption of bone matrix by non-carnivores to obtain minerals has been reported for ungulates (Yellen, 1977), red deer (Sutcliffe, 1973), caribou (Gordon, 1976), sheep (Brothwell, 1976), and rodents (Binford and Betram, 1977; Ubelaker, 1989). Insects and larvae may also cause displacement of bone even under conditions where other animal activity is not possible. Fungi and bacteria may also alter bone postmortem. Microradiographic evaluation of femur midshaft thin sections revealed nearly one-quarter to have postmortem alterations from fungi or bacteria. Several intrinsic processes of bone tissue, such as degree of mineralization and tunneling, appear to affect the likelihood of micro-organism activity (Hanson and Buikstra, 1987).

WEATHERING MODIFICATIONS TO BONE

It is often difficult to separate the processes of carnivore damage and natural weathering that occur in systemic context. Hill (1975) has investigated natural modern accumulations of animal bone found in a variety of contemporary environments (in which humans have not been directly involved) in Rwenzori and Kiberega National Parks, Uganda, and in Kenya, east of Lake Turkana (formerly Lake Rudolf), as part of the Koobi Fora Research Project.

Spiral fractures in bones subject to torsional stress (e.g., humeri, tibiae) occur as a result of natural weathering. Small triangular sections of long bones may derive from such processes. Right-angle compressional fractures, parallel to and perpendicular to the long axis of bone, may also occur by weathering (Gifford, 1981). Broken lower borders of mandibles are frequent and most commonly due to natural weathering processes. A characteristic deep crack, parallel to the horizontal axis of the ramus, appears early in the weathering process and may ultimately result in a sharp break lateral to the mandibular canal at the junction of the basal and alveolar portions of the mandible. The ascending ramus of the mandible is often lost in a similar manner.

Bone weathering has also resulted in selective preservation of particular skeletal elements observed in human burials in Sierra Madre Occidental, New Mexico (Pastron and Clewlow, 1974). These remains had been sealed in caves, rock shelters and crevices with a rock wall, and cemented with mud and clay. Only those walls that had disintegrated were opened by the investigators. Selective preservation was considered to be a consequence of intrinsic decomposition and weathering alone, since it was felt that soft tissue would have been completely decayed by the time of exposure to the elements in the alternately wet and dry seasons of the Sierra Madre. All burials were essentially prehistoric, since the Spanish Church supplanted cave burial with cemetery burial. The femur was observed to be the most durable element, as the heaviest and most dense bone. After the femur, in order of decreasing survivability, were the long bones of the lower extremity, tibia and fibula, and the long bones of the upper extremity, humerus, ulna and radius. Among the long bones, distal articular ends were better preserved than proximal (Pastron and Clewlow, 1974), as also observed for the humerus due to carnivore damage (Binford, 1981:ch. 3). The overall tendency is for larger bones to survive more within an extremity, and for the lower extremity to survive more than the upper extremity, based upon weathering patterns. Whether the latter effect is strictly size-related has not been determined.

These findings are summarized in Table 21.

Table 21. Selective Preservation of Skeletal Elements by Weathering Processes

Bone	Survivability	Origin	Size
Femur	greatest	lower extremity	largest
Tibia			
Fibular			
Humerus		upper extremity	
Ulna			
Radius	least		smallest

Therefore, "survivability" based upon weathering processes alone contrasts to some extent with the patterns observed as a result of carnivore (Binford, 1981) and human (Yellen, 1977) activity, in that smaller bones are less survivable. Based upon scaling principles alone, smaller bones have a large surface-to-volume ratio and may be more subject to weathering on this basis.

Behrensmeyer (1975) has investigated the physical agents which cause non-organic weathering. Five "weathering stages" were defined, ranging from fresh bone to total disintegration, based upon a "nominal quartz grain diameter equivalent." The effects of diagnenesis on a group of skeletal remains from Roman forts in Europe (A.D. 100–400) were studied by Jambar (1988). Quantification of the degree of soil infiltration in the specimens led to the conclusion that titanium, cobalt and chrome levels indicate the degree of surface contamination, and levels of manganese, potassium and lithium indicate the degree of ion permeability of the bone. In arid environments, bleaching, cortical breakdown and exfoliation of bone due to weathering appears at approximately nine months exposure time (Galloway et al., 1989). These changes may indicate the beginning stages of destruction of the skeletal elements. Specimens buried deep in the earth exhibit marked diffuse erosion which shows the classical appearance of fungi activity. Sea-immersed specimens show only superficial attack by micro-organisms (the antibacteral effect of saline aqueous solutions is well known). Bone specimens immersed in fresh water show patterns intermediate between earth burial and water immersion. Apatite has been found as the bone mineral substance in earth, sea and lake immersed bones. The amount of hydroxyproline as related to the weight of bone powder is diminished only in those areas corresponding to erosion by biological agents (Arnaud et al., 1980).

TRANSPORT OF BONE

The dispersion and concentration of bones is determined by both antemortem and postmortem processes, due to both human and non-human activities (Binford, 1978; Gifford, 1981). Biotic factors of antemortem processes have been discussed by Grey (1973). Relevant postmortem processes affecting final deposition of bone are biological (e.g. carnivore bone collecting) and geological (e.g. flowing water). Animals are rarely trapped naturally, or preserved where they lay down and died.

Bones may be transported, or as secondary "riders" in phoretic associations. Selective transport of bone depends upon the size, density and other features of a bone, and may provide correlation information in archaeologic context. Selective transport may also lead to information in archaeologic context. Selective transport may also lead to information losses. Brain (1969, 1981) has distinguished bone assemblage patterns due to (1) human consumption of animals, (2) carnivore consumption of bones, and (3) non-carnivore trampling of bones. These extrinsic processes all result in patterns which differ from each other, and from intrinsic natural processes, provided the assemblages are *not* subject to selective transport. The form, and corresponding function, of bone determines both its appeal to carnivores and its behavior as a sedimentary particle.

In addition to movement of partially or completely skeletonized remains by carnivore activity, other agents may cause transport of remains prior to deposition or after burial resurfacing. Voorhies (1969) has divided surface bones into "transport groups," based upon size and shape, but such scales are not fully useful because prior sequences of decay and disarticulation determine which components become available for individual transport at what point in time. Boaz and Behrensmeyer (1976) attempted to construct a useful index for the transport behavior of human skeletal parts in water flowing in a stream or river. Behaviors of bone in flowing water include sliding, flipping, rolling, and stable or quasi-stable. Skeletal parts can be differentiated into distinct groups of lag and transportable elements. There may be variation within a bone, e.g., complete crania are rapidly transported (due to buoyancy) while cranial fragments lag.

Density is primarily correlated with the rate of movement of a bone in flowing water; the denser the bone, the less transportable. Wet weight in air, weight in water and volume are not correlated with transportability. The density of a bone determines both its transportability and survivability. Therefore, a denser bone is more likely to persist at a site for reasons of both transportability and survivability. It is less likely to be destroyed by attritional agents on site, and it is less likely to be transported away. The effect of transport on breakage is important to construction of an integrated index of on-site survivability. If transport contributes to fragmentation, denser bones with inherent resistance to breakage will also not be exposed to breakage in transport.

Information regarding transport helps to determine the nature of skeletal assemblages as authochthonous (deposited where the human or animal died) or allochthonous (transported and deposited away from the primary site). Hanson (1980) has reviewed fluvial taphonomic processes.

EFFECTS OF SOIL DISTURBANCE
PROCESSES ON POSTMORTEM REMAINS

Once bone enters the archaeologic soil matrix it is subjected to a number of soil disturbance processes, or pedoturbation. Dynamic soil processes influence the deposition and placement of remains. These agents of attrition are quantitative vectors in that they have both magnitude and direction. The archaeologic matrix in which postmortem remains are embedded forms a system in which dynamics of soil formation and distribance processes exercise a major influence.

Soil Formation Processes

Soil formation results from horizonation, homogenization (haploidization) and pedoturbation or "soil mixing" (Hole, 1961), with biological, chemical and physical changes. The formation of vertisols, or "self-swallowing" soils, occurs through the alteration of wet and dry cycles and actions of expansile soil clays. Vertisols are dynamic soils which may disrupt stratigraphic sequences and archaeologic context. These soils are not well suited to agriculture, and specific geographic distributions within the United States and around the world have been determined (Duffield, 1970). Various soil organisms participate in the creation of soil, such as the earthworm. In one of his earliest performed but last published works, Charles Darwin investigated the soil-forming activities of earthworms in Roman ruins in England (*The Formation of Vegetable Mould Through the Action of Worms*, 1881). Creation of vermiborolls, vermudolls and vermustolls occurs through the action of earthworms. These processes may involve soil disturbance, as well as soil formation.

Soil Disturbance Processes

Faunalturbation may also occur through the action of burrowing mammals, crayfish and insects such as ants and termites, as well as earthworms. Floral alteration may occur by the action of plants. Root casts lead to the creation of krotovina-like structures in soil, and "wind throw" or tree fall contributes to the creation of a cradle-knoll topography. At the Dutch Mesolithic site of Bergumermeer, Newell and Musch (Gifford, 1978) have discerned evidence of "treefall" interspersed with evidence of actual structures. These two types of features differ in shape and placement, and with respect to artifacts found within. It is possible that some of the hearthless "huts" and "tent circles" in forested areas of Northern Europe (Rust, 1943) are actually the remains of ancient treefalls.

No studies have been attempted to determine the rate of root penetration into buried bones or to bones left on the surface. In temperate climate zones, penetration of plant roots into bone is rare, unless a burial is within range of rapidly growing trees, such as locust trees (Stewart, 1979:75). In tropical climate zones, plants grow rapidly and may destroy any bones within reach before final deposition (Warren, 1975, 1980).

Cryoturbation is soil disturbance by freeze-thaw action which also affects postmortem disposition of remains independently (Micozzi, 1986). This phenomenon is dependent upon the water content of soil and occurs in Arctic, montane and mid-latitude regions where there is frozen ground. Continuous and discontinuous permafrost zones cover 25 percent of the surface of the earth, while seasonally frozen ground covers 50 percent.

Soil, like water, freezes from the surface downward. Freezing causes expansion of water, and hence soil, by conformational changes in H_2O crystal molecules at $4°$ C. Soil freezing has the same effect on capillarity as does surface evaporation of soil water, and the actual expansion of soil is even greater with freezing due to this effect. Ice heaving occurs due to frost pull or push depending upon the heat conductivity of bone in relation to soil. These freezing processes may result in several features: heaved soil and up-freezing of bone, mass displacement and involution, cracking and wedging, sorting and ground patterning into circles, polygons, nets, steps and stripes.

Graviturbation includes solifluction, gelifluction (permafrost solifluction), mass wasting (creep solifluction) and glacial activity not related to the freeze-thaw cycle. Argilliturbation is expansion and contraction of hydrophilic clays, usually occurring in seasonally wet and dry tropical and subtropical regions. Aeroturbation is due to the actions of soil gas or wind and is responsible for the creation of "desert pavement" and contributes to the tree fall, or "wind throw" of floraturbation. Aquaturbation includes artesian and cryostatic-hydrostatic influences and may be considered to include fluvial transport of resurfaced remains after deposition. Crystalturbation occurs in subhumid regions and is due to the growth and dissolution of soil salts. Seismiturbation is cataclysmic alteration and disturbances due to the action of earthquakes. A general summary and time course of these processes is shown in Table 22.

Different geographic regions are subject to these processes to varying extents, and a site-specific index of pedoturbation may be developed with respect to climate, rainfall, seasonality, latitude and other factors. The predominance of these processes may be estimated for a given site at a given time spatially, but the temporal diachronic dimension must be added to determine changes in climate with time. Various combinations of processes may lead to specific feature formation in various regions. "Fingerprint topography" and linear gilgai occur in subtropical regions due to a combination of argilloturbation and graviturbation processes. Gelifluction lobes occur at high latitudes and altitudes due to the action of graviturbation, cryoturbation and secondary aquaturbation. Deserts are susceptible to argilliturbation and aeroturbation.

In addition to specific cryoturbative processes, whether or not a region is subject to frost qualitatively and quantitatively alters the character of many other pedoturbative processes. In frost zones, graviturbation will be manifest as gelifluction (rather than solifluction), as well as soil creep. Aquaturbation will be differentially manifest as cryostatic rather than artesian processes. (Table 23). The occurrence of these various specific topographic features at a given site may help identify the soil pedoturbative processes in operation over time.

There may also be subregional, site-specific variations in pedoturbative processes based upon topography and drainage. Cryoturbation causes resurfacing, while faunalturbation causes burial. In well-drained soils, faunal will predominate over cryoturbation, while in poorly-drained soils, the opposite will pertain (to which must be added the effects of crayfish, etc.) (Table 24). As a result of all these processes, remains may alternatively sink into soil, concentrate into layers at various depths, become reoriented, thrust to the surface, or move horizontally on a plane, or downslope, within soil. Processes occurring in short time-frame windows are superimposed upon the substrate of more gradual activities, and instantaneous events (seismiturbation) and rapid processes (graviturbation) are superimposed upon both.

Table 22. Pedoturbation Processes by Spatial and Temporal Dimensions

Process	Vectors (direction & magnitude)	Spatial Dimension	Time Dimension	Results Features
Faunalturbation	Animals*			
	1) burrowing mammals, crayfish	wide distribution water margins discontinuous	decades	resurfacing
	2) microfauna soc. insects earthworms	wide wide	years years	resurfacing burial
	3) megafauna	high plains	cntrys	deflation and solution
Floralturbation	Plants* root casts (plus wind) treefall	forests	500–1000 yrs.	burial resurfacing
Cryoturabation	soil; water freeze-thaw	Arctic Montane mid-latitude	several freeze-thaw cycles	differential upward, lateral displacement
Graviturbation	mass wasting	periglacial	centuries 3 cm/yr	horizontal and downward displacement
Aeroturbation	gas, air, wind	deserts	variable	deflation "telescoping"
Aquaturbation	water	middle & high latitudes	variable	involution and displacement
Crystalburbation	mineral salts	subhumid regions	gradual	dispersal
Seismiturbation	earthquakes volcanic erupt	fault zones	instantaneous instantaneous	cracking, shifting "systemic burial"
Argilliturbation	clays	seasonally wet & dry tropics and sub-tropics	gradual	vertical churning

*Species-specific range

Table 23. Regional Variations in Pedoturbative Processes

Region	Process Combination	Results & Features
Semi-tropical	Argilliturbation Graviturbation	"Fingerprint" topography Linear gilgai
High altitudes and latitudes	Graviturbation Cryoturbation Aquaturbation	Gelifluction lobes
Deserts	Argilliturbation Aeroturbation	Desert pavement Gibber plains Vesiculation
Forest	Floralturbation	Cradle knoll topography Burial

Table 24. Site Specific Variations in Pedoturbative Processes

Drainage	Processes	Results
Well-drained sites	Faunalturbation > Cryoturbation	Burial > Resurfacing
Poorly-drained sites	Cryoturbation > Faunalturbation (and effects of crayfish)	Resurfacing > Burial

Chapter VIII

ARCHAEOLOGIC THEORY, METHODOLOGY AND APPLICATIONS OF TAPHONOMY

HUMAN BEHAVIOR AND MATERIAL REMAINS

Archaeology may be defined as the study of human behavior and material culture. The manner in which activities in systemic context result in the creation of material in archaeologic context is critical to the perception and reconstitution of human behavior. All human behavior in archaeologic context is seen through the lens of taphonomic transformation. Taphonomic transformation results in the mechanical alteration of the objects of material culture itself. It is useful to determine by what processes objects in systemic context come to have a specific morphology and demonstrate particular spatial relationships in archaeologic context.

Schiffer (1976) demonstrates different temporal transformational strategies for study of the relations between human behavior and material culture. Past material culture may be used for the study of past human behavior. Present material culture may be used to reconstruct patterns of past human behavior, a study which has been called "experimental archaeology," "living archaeology," or "ethnoarchaeology." Past material culture may also be used to understand present human behavior. Finally, present material culture may be used to study present human behavior, or urban archaeology, as in the "project du garbage" of Rathje (1982). The synchronic study of past material-past behavior and present material-present culture may be considered nomothetic, in which specific associations and cause-and-effect laws may be experimentally detected, determined and documented. The diachronic study of past material-present behavior and present material-past behavior are ideographic in that they attempt to apply archaeologic principles across the boundaries of time and space to explanatory models.

The synthetic model of archaeology recognizes material in a static spatial relationship ("fossil" culture) as output from a cultural system subjected to non-cultural processes. The behavioral meaning of cultural material is thus transformed to spatial meaning in the archaeologic record. Binford (1964) has described material culture in archaeologic context as a localized record of the actual operation of an extinct society. Schiffer (1976) cautions that these archaeologic facts do not "speak for themselves," but have been subjected to a number of regular processes which may alter material culture spatially, quantitatively, formally and relationally (Collins, 1975). Such processes are termed C-(cultural) and N-(natural) transforms. These processes must be taken into account in order to understand the manner in which human behavior in a past cultural system results in the creation of material culture in the archaeologic record. The C-transform relates primarily to differential deposition of cultural material into archaeologic context and helps predict what material may be deposited by a system. N-transforms are noncultural or natural formation processes which relate to differential survival of cultural materials in the archaeologic record. For example, pollen is preserved in acidic soil, but bone is destroyed by soil acids. The characterization of variables that affect differential deposition and survival of cultural material will allow prediction of the interaction of C- and N-transforms in creation of the archaeologic record.

Cultural formation processes create both contemporaneous materials in systemic context and past materials in archaeologic context. Cultural deposition results in transformation of cultural material from the systemic context to the archaeologic context (S–A process). Archaeologic material may be introduced back into systemic context through the operation of a number of transformational agents (A–S process). Material culture may be transformed from state to state within archaeologic context without participating in systemic context (A–A process), as in the effects of agriculture on soil (e.g., Redman and Watson, 1970). Cultural material may also be transformed from one systemic state to another, or used in successive systemic states, without entering archaeologic context, as with lateral cycling and recycling (S–S process). Study of these systemic transfer processes may be termed *ethnoarchaeology.* Formation and transformation processes with archaeologic significance are shown in Table 25.

Raw materials enter cultural context through patterned human behavior. Cultural elements subject to transformational processes may be considered to fall into three categories: durables, consumables and energy sources. Basic processes relating to the transformation of these elements are shown in Table 26. At each step of these procedures, S–A processes may operate.

Table 25. Formation and Transformation Processes

S–A Processes	S–S Processes	A–S Processes	A–A Processes
Normal	Lateral cycling	Scavenging	Agriculture
Discard	Formal	Animal	Construction
Primary refuse	Informal	Humans	
Secondary refuse	Recycling	Pothunting	
Loss		Construction	
Disposal of the dead		Curation	
Cachement			
Abandonment			
Catastrophe			

Table 26. Basic Processes of Transformation of Cultural Elements

Durables	Consumables	Energy Sources
Procurement	Procurement	Procurement
Manufacture	Preparation	
Use	Consumption	Consumption
Maintenance		
Discard	Discard	Discard
Transport		
Storage		

Schiffer (1976) describes a typical C-transform: butchery of an animal at a kill site results in fewer bones being carried back and discarded at the base camp, and he invokes the "schlepp" effect (Daly, 1969) as a C-transform. For Binford (1978), the Eskimo technique of butchering and determination of which parts are given to dogs would be a C-transform. To the extent that dogs are "natural carnivores," their subsequent behavior and actions on the bones may be considered N-transforms. The mechanical forces and corresponding alterations in morphology resulting from carnivore behavior will be patterned subject to natural laws. However, to the extent that these domesticated dogs are part of a cultural system, with spatial and temporal access to bones determined by human behavior, these activities may still be considered within the realm of cultural transformation.

Schiffer (1976) concentrates on the role of human behavior in all formation and transformation processes (e.g., even for A–A processes, which occur totally within archaeologic context, the reference is to agricultural activity). It is necessary to develop laws for N-transformation, as Schiffer has attempted to do for C-transformations. What Schiffer refers to as N-transforms are soil "disturbance" processes to Wood and Johnson (1978). These disturbance processes which depositionally affect culturally-transformed materials are important to taphonomy and may actually contribute information to the archaeologic record (Binford, 1978).

Binford (1981b) attempts to resolve this issue by using "middle range" theory to explain how relationships in the archaeologic record are created by C- and N-transforms. While Schiffer (1976) regards C-transforms as a distorting lens through which material (which is somehow intrinsically archaeologic) must pass, Binford argues that this material does not become part of the archaeologic record but by the operation of cultural transformation. The archaeologic record is not a distortion of past culture, but relations revealed in the archaeologic context actually demonstrate the dynamic operation of past culture. In this sense, C-transforms can not be called "distortions" of the archaeologic record since C-transforms are the result of the actual operation of a cultural system. The archaeologic record is a result of the "normal" operation of such systems.

Therefore, the characterization of N-transforms is critical to understanding the depositional distortions which occur to cultural material and to interpreting their meaning. The interaction of C- and N-transforms will, to a large extent, determine the preservation, patterning, survivability and recognizability ("visibility") of the archaeologic record. While C-transforms are the primary agency producing the remains which archaeologists study, and archaeologic research has focused mainly on gathering data to test hypotheses concerning the relations between the culture process and its material manifestations, additional N-transforms substantially alter the archaeologic record (Gifford, 1978). Natural processes affecting the deposition of cultural materials (Binford, 1974) may be applied specifically to the deposition of human and animal remains (Gifford, 1978).

INFORMATION GAINS FROM TAPHONOMY

The end-products appearing in the archaeologic record are the result of the dynamic interaction of organic remains and postmortem processes. While postmortem processes delete some information and introduce "bias" in the archaeologic record, patterns of assemblage also yield significant information about life processes (Gifford, 1981). The taphonomic agents of archaeologic bias are ecological in nature and operation. Taphonomy represents a dynamic interaction of bone and the archaeologic matrix. Further, bone actually becomes a part of the archaeologic matrix and, in turn, alters *it* (Binford, 1981). Taphonomic transformation may also lead to gains rather than losses in information for reconstruction of environment and behavior (Binford, 1981). The informational potential of taphonomy has been indicated in several areas of investigation.

Differential artefactual damage to bones due to age-dependent changes in density of bone matrix (Brain, 1969, 1980, 1981; Binford, 1981) may help determine the age structure of a population. Gnawing and total consumption of bone, beyond normal carnivore consumption patterns, may occur in environments where there are low levels of minerals and salts. This behavior has been reported for ungulates (Yellen, 1976), including red deer (Sutcliff, 1973), caribou (Gordon, 1976) and sheep (Brothwell, 1976), which are naturally non-carnivorous. Non-carnivores may also cause trampling damage to bone, not related to primary consumption, proportional to the size of living populations (Gifford, 1981) and size of the individual members of those populations. Non-carnivore, or carnivore, collectors of bone may transport bones to a greater extent than they actually "process" them (Thomas, 1971).

The extent of damage to bones by carnivores is related to their degree of hunger (Binford, 1978, 1981), which may be used as an index of nutrition with extrapolation to environmental conditions or changes. Conversely, nutritional status of a population, which may be age-dependent or demographic-ecologic, determines the composition and density of bone and in turn influences taphonomic patterns. Finally, small animal bones are more likely to be totally destroyed, since their surface area is proportionally greater than their volume (Dodson and Wexlar, 1979).

Each bone has a certain survival potential ("survivability") determined by specific gravity, according to Brain (1981) and density according to Binford (1977, 1978, 1981), which are proportional to each other. Thus, differential wear on different bones, and on different segments of the same bone, may be seen as an index of the "taphonomic stress" (e.g., "overburden") applied to a given bone in a skeleton, or to a given skeleton or skeletal element in an assemblage. Taphonomic stress results from contact of organic remains with attritional agents at various environmental interfaces. These "contacts" are dependent upon the various phases of transformation during which dynamic equilibrium systems may be determined. The types of bone damage (taphonomic traits) will depend upon the intrinsic character of bone (as determined by biotic factors) and the types of attritional agents acting (taphonomic processes) in that equilibrium system. Various forces may also push remains into one phase or another of transformation, causing entry into another closed equilibrium system. Contact with the environment may be made in soil by taphic factors, and at the surface by perthotaxic and anataxic factors. The dynamic properties of each system determine the sensitivity and specificity of specific taphonomic traits for distinctive taphonomic processes.

These two components of a dynamic equilibrium system can be related to Binford's (1981:ch.1) concept of integrity and resolution of an assemblage. The homogeneity of agents responsible for materials in a deposit (integrity) relate to *precision* of a system. The homogeneity of events or situations whose by-products appear in a deposit (resolution) relate to the *accuracy* of a system. The resolution of a system may be "fine-grained" as related to a record of instantaneous, short-term events; or "coarse-grained," representing an integrated index of cumulative, long-term processes. Some archaeologic assemblages with low "survivability" and attenuated archaeologic "visibility" may thus carry more information than do better preserved systems (Binford and Bertram, 1977). Thus, in assessing the effects of non-cultural processes on the archaeologic record, ethnoarchaeologic and taphonomic research may do more than simply provide *caveats* (Gifford, 1978).

STUDY DESIGN AND RATIONALE

The methodology of taphonomy involves definition of attritional processes which modify archaeologic assemblages (taphonomic processes), recognition of the resulting corresponding patterns, and extrapolation of this information back to the archaeologic record for interpretive use (Binford and Bertram, 1977). This methodology consists of actualistic research designed to determine the ecological meanings of patterns in assemblages of biological remains, establish the role of remains as components of ecosystems, and distinguish human patterns from "bone processing" by carnivores and other attritional agents (Gifford, 1981). The methodology includes the use of contemporary isomorphic analogues to guide interpretation under the principles of uniformitarianism. Thus, both observations of contemporary processes in the present and analysis of prehistoric evidence from the past may be used to understand past processes.

Confrontation of the archaeologic record with knowledge of present processes may be termed "actualism" (Gifford, 1981). Binford (1981:ch.3) also describes the research methodology for construction of "middle-range" theory as actualistic, through demonstration of cause-and-effect relationships. Binford suggests several investigative strategies. Ethno-archaeology of living systems allows direct observation of cause and effect. Experimental archaeology seeks to replicate relevant dynamics of the study situation in order to directly demonstrate cause and effect. Historical archaeology allows cause-and-effect relationships to be discerned where relevant dynamics are recorded or documented.

Consistent with the goal of construction of "middle-range" theory, Binford and Bertram (1977) attempt in-depth explanation of the operation of single attritional processes in isolation in order to discover general principles of taphonomic transformation. For the purposes of experimental archaeology, there is a requirement for well-controlled archaeologic assemblages with known agents of attrition and relevant characteristics of "survivability" for bone populations. In his ethno-archaeologic studies of Nunamiut Eskimo dogs, Binford (1971) initially observed final conditions but did not know initial conditions. Then, he established initial conditions but had no controlled observations for final condition (Binford, 1978). Finally, he established initial and final conditions for demonstration of cause-and-effect relationships (Binford, 1981). He thus determined that dogs modify the character of skeletal assemblages in a systematic manner, and that survival of parts after the operation of an agent of attrition was not proportionate to the representation of the original assemblage. This patterned destruction raised the issue of archaeologic visibility (survivability and recognizability) as a limiting factor, since there is conservation of mass in any closed equilibrium system.

Binford and Bertram (1977) establish experimental parameters to determine "survivability" as a function of bone density, which varies by age, species and nutritional status. Once established, a reverse index of controlled survivability of remains may be related back to nutritional and demographic-ecologic factors, in turn, albeit in a somewhat tautological exercise. They then attempt objective measurement of the strength of physical, chemical and biological agents of attrition acting on bone, beyond or porosity of bone per se. Thus, survival of bone also relates to the strength of attritional agents acting over time.

APPLICATION OF TAPHONOMY

Human behavior may be reconstructed from faunal remains in depositional context. However animal and human remains are likely to undergo a number of postmortem transformations that do not affect non-organic artifacts (e.g., stone tools, pots). Binford (1981) has said simply that "faunal remains are not stone tools." While it can generally be accepted that no agencies other than patterned human behavior can account for the presence of stone tools and pottery, several processes operate on bone which prevent the assignation of humans as the unequivocal agents of change. A central question to taphonomy and paleontology has been how to recognize the products of hominid human behavior in faunal remains, and to determine the degree of association of stone tools and bones with human behavior. The hierarchy of units of archaeologic study, including artifacts, assemblages, sites and habitats, are all subject to taphonomic transformation. The recent past has relied upon an associational perspective, using the concept of habitation, to ascribe faunal assemblages to human behavior. Postmortem modification of human and animal remains occurs in systematic fashion. Recognition of the patterns resulting from various modalities of postmortem modification permits differentiation of human behavior from other transformations. Binford (1981) has identified several operational definitions in archaeology useful in taphonomy. The original operational definition of humans as "toolmakers" placed reliance upon archaeologic evidence in the form of relics and monuments. Evidence that bipedalism, with freeing of hands, proceeded other hominid evolutionary developments (Lovejoy, 1981) has significance to this definition.

A more recent operational definition of what Binford (1981) has called "man-the-homemaker" has placed reliance on artifacts and skeletal assemblages, drawn from contemporary experience. The underlying assumptions of this definition have been that all aggregations of relics were assembled through human activity, all animal bones represent the remains of human meals, all fires were lit by humans and everything that happened in "sheltered settings" involved humans. This operational definition of a human "living floor" as any aggregation of artifacts (relics) on a land surface, without regard for soil disturbance processes, was a corollary to the "man-the-homemaker" hypothesis.

However, it has been realized that a variety of activities by predators, scavengers and non-organic agents may mask human activities by sheer overwhelming numbers (Binford, 1981). Isaac and Isaac (1975:17) have conjectured that several early hominid behaviors took place from about three million years ago, based upon the association of stone tools with animal bones in the archaeologic record. Meat eating was regularly practiced, and persistent hunting almost certainly took place. Localities at which both discarded tools and bone refuse accumulated are more readily explained as home bases in the distinctive sense. The consumption of food at a home base involves transporting food from the place where it was obtained. The quantities that can be estimated suggest far more food was transported than was needed for feeding infants; thus extensive sharing seems an inevitable conclusion.

Leakey (1971) recognized the limitations of drawing such inferences from the archaeologic record and developed criteria for accepting deposits as "occupational floors" of four basic classes:

(1) living floors—occupational debris found on a paleosol, or old land surface, with avertical distribution only a few centimeters,

(2) kill and butchering sites—artifacts associated with the skeleton of large mammal or with a group of smaller animals,

(3) diffuse sites—artifacts and faunal remains distributed through a considerable depth of clay as fine-grained toff (vertisol),

(4) riverine and stream channel sites—hominid debris incorporated in the filling at a former river or stream channel.

However, archaeologic investigations of bones have been characterized by incorrect association of human artifacts with bone, incorrect assignment of human behavior as responsible for all changes in an archaeologic site, incorrect identification of the agents responsible for change, and incorrect assumption of mass causality for all changes. The uniformitarian assumption is that the same factors which determine natural conditions may also operate on bone in either a directed or non-specific manner (Binford, 1981:ch. 4).

While the bones of animals at archaeologic sites may represent food (Daly, 1969; Yellen, 1977), faunal assemblages result not only from human activities but also from the activities of other animals, as well as intrinsic processes of decay (Payne, 1965; Micozzi, 1986). Recognizing variability within human behavior is also part of the process of distinguish ing human from other sources of artifact in the archaeologic record. Variability in butchering techniques may be based upon idiosyncratic preferences of individuals operating within a defined cultural system or contingent upon variable factors which may be known and quantified. Individualized food preferences may or may not arise within a cultural system (Binford, 1981:39).

The influence of external physical conditions as limiting factors on human behavior may be applied to any culture, if environment and seasonality are defined. The influence of the social environment, such as ethnicity, size and structure of population groups, may be discerned within any physical environment or season when relevant cultural variables are defined. Furthermore, the influence of all "generalizing" factors of physical and social environment will leave an imprint upon which of the "specifying" factors of human behavior, regarding procurement of food, shelter or tools, are being superimposed.

Seasonal effects and physical conditions may influence both cultural and natural transformation of bones. For C-transforms, Binford (1978) describes that natural freezing of meat determines the pattern of butchering employed by Nunamiut Eskimos. Freezing also affects natural decay patterns (Micozzi, 1986). While these patterns may perhaps give indirect evidence of seasonality, it is also possible to objectively determine the season of death of mammals by examination of tooth remains in the archaeologic site (Bourque and Morris, 1975).

Identifying and distinguishing the effects of human butchering from other agents of change requires an understanding of cultural processes related to subsistence patterns. Butchering is in reality a task of dismemberment (Binford, 1978:61), which does not destroy bone but disorganizes the anatomy. Since butchery is essentially disarticulation, the extent to which it is possible to distinguish natural from human processes, and the actions of human or hominid carnivores from other carnivore predators and scavengers, is strongly influenced by taphonomic principles.

A typical sequence of dismemberment in butchery by the Nunamiut Eskimo is given by Binford (1981:ch. 4). Nunamiut butchery is characterized by division into discrete sets of anatomical parts: (1) antlers, skull, mandible; (2) altas, axis and vervical vertebrae; (3) thoracic vertebrae and first two ribs, bilaterally; (4) sternum and costal ribs; (5) ribs/slabs (10 ribs each); (6) front legs; (7) rear legs. The use of anatomical parts may be conditioned by the manner in which the carcass is dismembered, or the manner of dismemberment may determine the use of the parts. Conversely, the intended use of the animal may determine the manner of dismemberment. There are discrete differences in the anatomical segments observed to result from "natural" processes of decay and disarticulation (Hill, 1975).

The typical stages of animal butchery and processing include skinning, evisceration, disarticulation, filleting, fracture (marrow consumption) and possible burning. The primary activities of butchery are located in the field and timed or scheduled based upon hunting and killing activities. Secondary activities occur back at "camp" and involve storage, distribution and consumption of derived food. There may be diagnostic patterns of articulation, part association and inflected cut marks for each specific activity. These patterns may help locate the specific functions of each site. For carnivores, major anatomical disorganization can be expected to occur at the primary place of consumption, which is spatially the same place as the kill site. Human patterns will be based upon a "general utility index" (Binford, 1981:ch. 5) of the differential value of a given anatomical part. What humans choose to preferentially transport away from the kill site for later consumption at the "base camp" are just those parts which carnivores generally leave at the site, having preferentially consumed them. Factors which determine preferential consumption of anatomic parts are the same for all carnivores, both human and non-human, and specifically determine what is taken away, by humans, but also what is left on site by other carnivores. The general utility index will further determine differential destruction in butchering, differential abandonment of parts during transport, and end-stage introduction of anatomic parts as non-foods (tools) by humans.

While a utility index is relevant to the intrinsic properties of organic remains which determine their behavior in a closed system, specifying factors influence the specific behavior of the agents of change which operate upon these remains. More extensive feeding activities lead to greater disarticulation and dispersal of remains as an index of carnivore behavior (Binford, 1981:ch. 5), which may in turn be associated with seasonal, nutritional and demographic-ecologic effects. Thus, patterned skeletal assemblages may appear in the archaeologic record for multiple causes.

To determine how overall patterns of human behavior participate in the creation of assemblages of given composition, Binford (1981) analyzed faunal remains and horizontal distributions of fauna and tools recovered from the stratified Mousterian site of Combe Grenal. Although the number of animals represented in any one occupation zone is relatively small, there were clear differences in the relative frequencies of anatomical parts of various animal species. Table 27 is constructed to summarize Binford's finds for the representation of animal parts for bovids and horses. Bovids and horses are represented by analogous anatomical parts and are clearly differentiated from reindeer and deer in parts present.

Table 27. Representation of Animal Parts at Combe Grenal

	Hererogeneity Index	*Frequent*	*Variable*	*Rare*
Bovids	small	mandibular, lower teeth, tibia, femur, humerus, ulna		ribs, vertebrae, pelvis, skull, metapodials, phalanges
Horses	small	mandibular, lower teeth, tibia, femur, humerus, ulna	maxillary teeth	ribs, vertebrae, pelvis, skull, metapodials, phalanges

The patterns of deer and reindeer bones are not as similar to each other as are the remains of bovids and horses. However, the similarities are such that they may be considered separately. There is greater variability in parts represented in different occupation sites, including assemblages analogous to those noted on kill sites (Dibble and Lorain, 1968; Kehoe, 1967; White, 1954) and to recognized patterns for semi-permanent settlements on the North American plains (Wood, 1962). No sites showed representation of anatomical parts in proportions to their appearance in the living skeleton. Dart (1957) found marked disproportions in skeletal parts associated with Australopithecine remains and interpreted these differences as due to hunting and tool-using behavior.

The excavation of Suberde in Turkey (ca. 6750 B.C.) by Bordaz (1970) provided one of the first archaeologic collections suitable for analysis of faunal remains (Daly, 1969). All animals bones were saved and each specimen recorded separately with the Termatrex System (Bordaz and Bordaz, 1966). Thus, anomalies in the collection were shown to be inherent and not artefactual. Perkins and Daly (1968) reported on the fauna from Suberde, and investigated the relative frequencies of anatomical parts recovered from several species. They observed that bones of the upper legs were underrepresented compared to the bones of the lower legs in bovids. Chaplin (1969) reported similar findings from a Saxon site near London. Explanations offered to account for different interspecies and intraspecies representation of anatomical parts at archaeologic sites are summarized in Tables 28 through 30.

Table 28. Differential Representation of Anatomical Parts Within Species within Site

(1) Butchering	differential destruction of parts (Dart, 1957; Kitching, 1963; White, 1953, 1954)
(2) Transport	differential transport of anatomical parts from kill sites to sites of consumption (Dibble and Lorain, 1968; Kehoe, 1967; Perkins and Daly, 1968; White, 1952)
(3) Consumption	differential destruction of anatomical parts during consumption by humans. direct consumption of soft bone parts (Brain, 1969; Kehoe, 1967; White, 1954) destruction of bone for extraction of "bone grease" (Kehoe, 1967; White, 1953)
(4) Scavenging	differential on-site destruction by domesticated dogs in base camps (Brain, 1969; Dibble and Lorain, 1968; White, 1954) differential on-site destruction by non-domesticated carnivores at kill sites (Brain, 1969; Kitching, 1963; Voorhies, 1969)
(5) Technology	removal or destruction of parts as a function of their use as tools or raw materials for tools (Dart, 1957; Kitching, 1963; White 1953)
(6) Trade	Differential transport of parts away from sites of consumption in the context of trade (Chaplin, 1969)

Table 29. Differential Representation of Anatomic Parts Between Species Within a Site

(1) Butchering	differential destruction of parts from different species as a function of differences in the size and strength of analogous anatomical parts (White, 1954) differential degree of butchering of different species at kill sites as a function of their size and transportability (White, 1953, 1954)
(2) Transport	differences between domesticated and wild forms, resulting in domesticated forms being butchered at the site of consumption and wild forms being butchered at kill sites (Perkins and Daily, 1968; White, 1954)
(3) Consumption	differential food preferences for analogous parts from different species (White, 1952)

Klein (1980) has discussed the differential survival of anatomical parts of animals of different species in South Africa, and Crader (1974) has described differential representation and preservation of individual bone elements due to actions of predators and scavengers. Brain (1969) demonstrated that the survival of identifiable bones varied directly with the specific gravity of the part and inversely with the fusion time of the articular

Table 30. Differential Representation of Anatomical Parts Within Species Between Sites

(1) Butchering	functional differences between the sites, e.g. kill sites vs. village sites (Clark and Haynes, 1970; Dibble and Lorain, 1968; Kehoe, 1967; White, 1952)
(2) Consumption	ethnic differences in food preferences and consumption practices between the social groups represented at different sites (Dibble and Loran, 1968; Kehoe, 1967; White, 1954; Wood, 1962)

ends, and suggested that most of Dart's discrepancies in the Makapansgat fauna could be explained as a function of the differential durability of bones subjected to natural transformations. Voorhies (1969) has also observed differential frequencies of animal anatomic parts in an early Pliocene deposit in North America, long before human behavior could have been a factor, and ascribed these discrepancies to the activities of carnivores, differential sorting by natural agents, and differential destruction of parts as a function of their intrinsic properties of strength, density and specific gravity.

Through examination of nearly 20,000 hominid and animal fossils from the classic cave site of Sterkfontein, Swartkrans and Kromdraai, S. A., Brain (1981) demonstrated that early hominids were hunted by powerful predators (the great cats), and that it was only in the early Pleistocene Period that human technology developed to the point of reversing the balance. In faunal analysis of "living floors," Grayson (1978) stressed the importance of distinguishing the bone remains of a human meal from the human remains of an animal meal.

The detection of animal exploitation by humans is influenced by taphonomy not only in patterns of butchery at an immediate level, but in distinguishing what constitutes a domestic animal at a more general level in the cultural process. Osteologic evidence for domestication is usually scant and splintered; rarely is an articulated or partial skeleton found. Most non-osteologic evidence is not preserved in archaeologic remains. Thus, zooarchaeology or archaeozoology strongly needs interpretative taphonomic information (Olsen, 1978).

Chaplin (1969) pointed out that anatomic information may be of limited value for detection of domestication (e.g., postcranial remains of sheep and goat are virtually indistinguishable). The changes effected by domestication may be present in only a few bones of the body, which may in turn be subject to various transformations which preclude their preservation. Thus, the archaeologic context of the bones may generate more information than their morphology per se. Among Chaplin's factors for distinguishing domesticates in context are species, age, sex and size of animals, all of which are related to density and differential survivability of bone. Thus, while individual morphologic traits associated with domestication may not be preserved, differential taphonomic transformation of remains may actually lead to information gains in context. Archaeologically, domestication is only one pattern of animal exploitation by humans, including hunting and animal "management."

The detection of patterns of human exploitation of the environment is based upon the two consumption strategies for carnivores of moving consumers to goods, or goods to consumers. Binford (1981) distinguished human groups by their exploitation patterns as "foragers" or "collectors," with specific subsistence-settlement strategies that have significance for the detectable types of archaeologic deposition that result (Binford, 1980). Foragers, as characterized by Taylor (1964), have a residential base around water but move to localities where discrete activities of food procurement occur, e.g., kill sites. This behavior has been described as "tethered nomadism." Collectors are logistically organized around food procurement points and have shortage of food for at least part of the year.

Murdock (1967) recognized intermediate forms of hunter-gatherer settlement systems with (1) fully migratory or nomadic bands, (2) seminomadic-seasonal, (3) semisedentary-shifting fixed settlements, and (4) permanent compact settlements. Binford (1980) makes distinctions between these types of hunter-gatherer settlement systems for archaeologic site formations representing (1) residential base camp, (2) "location," (3) field camp, and (4) station (e.g., observation site) or cache. Potts and Walker (1981) present the production of early hominid archaeologic sites in terms of energetic conditions. They distinguish activity types represented as occupation sites, butchering stations, "factory" sites and food-sharing locations with respect to transport of organic remains for butchery and/or consumption. They conclude that complex social conditions are not required to explain archaeologic site patterns.

Paleontology has broadened its focus on the study of human evolution to include non-hominid vertebrate and invertebrate studies in an effort to establish or elucidate evolutionary principles which may equally apply to all species of life on earth. Taphonomy increases the ability to reliably interpret archaeologic information for application in these diverse areas.

Chapter IX

TAPHONOMY AND THE STUDY
OF DISEASE IN ANTIQUITY:
THE CASE OF CANCER

Taphonomic transformations postmortem influence what is available today to study in attempts to render a diagnosis of cancer or other disease in antiquity.

MODERN REFERENCES TO ANCIENT CANCERS

Many medical textbooks begin with words to the effect that cancer has been known since earliest times ... etc. Current publications such as the National Cancer Institute's *Closing in on Cancer: Solving a 5000-Year-Old Mystery* (1987) make statements such as, "Cancer is older than man, stalking dinosaurs long before the earliest written records document its ravages among humans." Such statements are based, for example, upon Egyptian medical papyri dating from 3000 B.C. making reference to what has been translated by nineteenth century Victorian Egyptologists without medical training as "tumors"; or such statements will refer to descriptions by the great nineteenth century German pathologist, Doctor Rudolph Virchow, of cancer in bears from the Neanderthal period and earlier. However, modern medical texts and writings are not always sophisticated about taphonomy (the study of postmortem change) or paleopathology (the study of diseases in antiquity). Modern translations of Egyptian papyri, for example, often reveal not cancer at all, but "tumors" in the traditional Latin sense of the word "swelling" (which can be due to any of a number of causes); and the Neanderthal cancer in bone described by Rudolph Virchow is a healing bone fracture when subjected to modern analysis. There is little or no hard evidence of cancer in antiquity.

One could conclude on this basis that cancer in antiquity was not as common as it is today. A frequent counterargument is that cancer is primarily a disease of old age (increasing age-specific rates observed for

91

most cancers in modern populations), and since people did not live to old age in antiquity, they did not live long enough to get cancer. Yet, the most and best preserved human remains from antiquity are primarily in the form of bone, and primary bone cancer is more common in the young than in the old. If bone neoplasia were common in antiquity, we should observe it in ancient bones in the form of osteochondroma, fibrous dysplasia, giant-cell tumor, histiocytosis X, Ewing's tumor and osteosarcoma in younger age groups. Regarding soft tissue remains to detect other cancers, Egyptian mummies provide an abundant source of preserved soft tissues. Wealthier ancient Egyptians had better, and more expensive, funerary preparations and are differentially represented among ancient mummified remains. Many also lived to advanced old age consistent with their better economic status. If cancer were common in antiquity, we should be able to detect it in ancient (and older) mummies.

WHY STUDY CANCER IN ANTIQUITY?

Recent epidemiologic observations are consistent with the possibility that 80–90 percent of human cancer may be due to environmental exposures, and that up to 30–40 percent of cancer can be explained by human diet and nutrition.

In light of current observations on variations in life-style, diet and cancer patterns in human populations around the world, there has been increasing interest in establishing synchronic relations between adaptational changes in nutritional patterns and changes in the rates of certain cancers that accompany modernization and westernization among human populations (Oiso, 1975). Numerous migrant studies (Albanes, Schatzkin and Micozzi, 1987) suggest that acculturation of diet and life-style among various migrant groups to the United States, coming from home populations with low incidence rates of certain cancers, is accompanied by increases in the rates of these cancers toward those of the host country. Acculturation is the process by which the dietary and other behaviors of migrant populations become similar to those of the host country.

Dietary and life-style patterns of human populations that have changed through time are also thought to have significant implications for the health of human populations (Eaton and Konner, 1985; Rathje and Ho, 1988). Development of a diachronic perspective on the antiquity of cancer in human populations undergoing demographic transition provides additional descriptive information about the possible influences of diet, life-style and other environmental factors on cancer through time.

HOW THE ANTIQUITY OF CANCER CAN BE STUDIED

Three types of descriptive observations are available to help build a diachronic perspective on the antiquity of cancer. The first category of evidence comes from human and animal remains, consisting primarily of skeletal remains that may or may not have undergone diagenesis (fossilization), as well as significant accumulations of soft tissue remains preserved through artificial or natural means, or combinations of the two. Selective preservation of such remains, as well as postmortem taphonomic transformations, and the morphologic appearance of such materials are important methodological considerations. Some of the so-called "fossil evidence" of ancient cancers reported by luminaries in the new field of anatomic pathology in the 1800s has not been born out as representing examples of malignancies when re-examined using modern techniques of diagnosis in the twentieth century and interpreted in light of postmortem transformations. However, the historic reports of the 1800s of "ancient cancers" have made their way into the modern textbooks, while the results of twentieth century re-analyses have been less visible in the secondary scientific literature.

Modern and early twentieth century populations around the world that had not undergone transition to a modern diet and life-style also provide a window on the relations of diet and health, as do modern primate populations, as well as other animal species in their natural habitats.

The second category of evidence comes from ancient clay tablets, papyri, texts and other documents which purportedly describe ancient cases of cancer therein. Again, many of these texts, initially preserved from antiquity by the Islamic civilizations of the late first and early second milleinae A.D., came under serious scrutiny in Europe in the late 1800s. These documents were often acquired by Victorian gentlemen who either translated or had them translated by scholars of antiquity with little or no medical or scientific background or training. The result is often scientifically uninformed (by then current standards) translation that is difficult to place into modern diagnostic or interpretive perspective.

Other literary and artistic depictions of disease have also led to speculation as to providing documentary evidence of cancers. Artistic and cultural representations from ancient civilizations have been interpreted as providing evidence for benign tumors and disorders such as osteomas, osteitis, osteochondroma and cranial meningioma; and possibly the malignant conditions of chondrosarcoma of the pelvis and naso-pharyngeal carcinoma.

The third category of evidence comes from early demographic and statistical information in populations when and where coincidentally (1) such data began to be collected, (2) cancer became recognized as a clinico-pathologic entity, and (3) cancer rates were observed to increase, in human populations. Such medical and vital statistics collected by the state for official purposes may or may not have been accompanied by data on employment, housing, life-style, nutrition, etc. Since increasing age is the greatest relative risk factor for most cancers, data on average life span and longevity are important to estimating age-specific rates of cancer in different historic populations.

PRESERVATION OF HUMAN AND ANIMAL REMAINS

Skeletal remains of biologic organisms, consisting of mineralized organic matrix, may be preserved postmortem under a variety of circumstances. The study of skeletal remains provides information on diseases of bone, as well as non-bone diseases, provided they leave the slightest traces on the skeleton (Dastugue, 1980). Common examples are skeletal morpho-logical changes associated with hematologic disorders, and reactive processes to meningioma, trauma of soft tissues, hemangiomas, aneurysms, and neurological disorders. With respect to the present analyses, skeletal remains also provide a permanent record of primary bone neoplasms, as well as metastatic cancers from other primary sites. This type of analysis does not permit consideration of diseases that leave no traces on bone, nor hypothetical diseases limited only to ancient populations leaving non-comparable or undecipherable traces in skeletons. However, the geologic law of uniformitarianism (Lyell, 1865) appears to apply to these studies as well. In any case of unequivocal diagnosis, all ancient diseases have appeared morphologically similar to their modern forms in over twenty years of paleopathological studies (Dastague, 1980). In cases of suspected or doubtful diagnoses, the uncertainty generally can be attributed to known variability within the manifestations of modern disease (Kelly and El-Najjar, 1980; Kelly and Micozzi, 1984). It seems reasonable to assume that if cancer exists in ancient skeletal remains, we should know what it looks like when subjected to modern analysis. Such remains can be subjected to modern techniques of clinical diagnosis, including roentgenography and other imaging studies, as well as gross, microscopic and ultrastructural pathologic analysis, as well as trace element studies. In fact, the x-ray appearance of pathologic findings in dry bone remains may be even more sensitive and specific than are x-ray studies on living humans (Micozzi, 1982; Ortner and Untermohle, 1981; Kelly and Micozzi, 1984).

In addition to the relatively commonplace preservation of human and animal skeletal remains, there are certain conditions under which soft tissues may also be preserved after death. Postmortem decay (aerobic) and decomposition (anaerobic) occurs in most environments due to chemical changes and microbial actions (Micozzi, 1986). However, if dehydration (desiccation) occurs rapidly prior to the onset of decay and decomposition, these chemical and biological changes can be arrested or indefinitely slowed. Postmortem preservation of tissue is essentially a competition between decomposition and desiccation. Desiccation occurs naturally due to environmental conditions commonly existing in the deserts of North Africa, Australia, the western coast of Chile and Peru, and the southwestern United States and northern Mexico. Desiccation can also be facilitated by cultural processes of evisceration and chemical treatment practiced by various populations throughout the world (see Chap. III).

Preservation of soft tissues also may occur under natural conditions, where tissues remain in which the diagnosis of cancer could be readily made if present (see Chap. II). Zimmerman (1977) has shown that malignant tumors from modern humans are well-preserved and recognizable in tissues experimentally subjected to processes that accurately reproduce environmental desiccation and tissue preservation. This experimental approach reproduces changes in non-malignant tissues that are identical to those observed in the preserved non-malignant remains of ancient individuals from a variety of sources, including Alaska, Egypt, etc. Also, experimental malignant tissues appear to be better preserved after desiccation than are non-malignant tissues. Metastatic tumors are also preserved and remain recognizable. Therefore, if physical evidence of cancer exists in ancient human and animal remains, it should be preserved and relatively recognizable within the bone or soft tissue remaining.

PALEOPATHOLOGIC EVIDENCE
FROM HUMAN AND ANIMAL REMAINS

Paleozoic and Mesozoic Eras

Primary malignancies of bone have not been positively identified among extinct animals (Brothwell and Sandison, 1967). The apparent absence of any recognizable diseases among animals of the early Paelozoic Era (195 to 520 million years B.C.) has also been commented upon (Brothwell and Sandison, 1967). The earliest example of a suspected neoplasm comes from the fossilized remains of a large dinosaur (genus *Apatosaurus*) from the Comanchean Period of the Mesozoic Era (70 to 195 million years B.C. by recent estimate) showing evidence of a benign hemangioma between two caudal vertebrae, a location showing similar predilections in modern humans (Swinton, in Hart, 1983; Coley, 1960). This specimen was collected from the Como beds, Comanchean Period of Wyoming by Doctor S. W. Williston at the time when these deposits were at the height of their fame as dinosaur quarries (Moodie, 1923).

The next oldest example is a benign osteoma involving the dorsal vertebra of a Mosasaurus from the later Cretaceous Period of the Mesozoic Era (Abel, 1924). Moodie (1923) and Lull (1933) also described suspected cases of "multiple myeloma" involving squamosal bones and adjunct maxillae in horned dinosaurs (*Torosaurus*) of the genus *Ceratopsia*. Swinton (1983) later reinterpreted the incorrect diagnosis of "multiple myeloma" in skulls of the *Ceratopsia*, writing that these lesions recall the fenestrae seen in later mammal and early human skulls which may be caused by a number of benign osteolytic processes. Finally, a dinosaur bone from Transylvania from 70 million years B.C. originally identified in a London Hospital as "periosteal sarcoma" was diagnosed in 1966 by Campbell (1966) as osteopetrosis.

Cenozoic Era

The Cenozoic Era comprises the Teritiary Period (Age of Mammals) and the Quaternary Period (Age of Humans) covering the last 70 million years to the present. As early as 1774, Doctor E. J. C. Esper (1742–1810) in Erlangen, Germany, described what he thought was an osteosarcoma in the distal femur of a cave bear (*Ursus spelaeus*) from the Pleistocene Period, as cited by Goldfuss (1810). However, this lesion was later described as a healing fracture callus with necrosis by Mayer (1854). Virchow's (1870, 1895, 1896) studies of the cave bears of Europe since the Middle

Teritiary Period were also well-known historically, but do not provide evidence of cancer in antiquity.

Perhaps the earliest example of a suspected malignant tumor in a hominid was described in the Kanam mandibular fragment from East Africa (Lawrence 1935), probably of the Lower or Middle Pleistocene (Brothwell, 1967). The details of the tumor are somewhat obscured by extensive diagenesis. The interpretation of this lesion by Tobias as a subperiosteal ossifying sarcoma has been accepted by Brothwell (1967), although there was some difference of opinion on this diagnosis. Goldstein (1969) also believed the lesion to be a "sarcomatous overgrowth." Finally, Stathopoulos (1975) suggested that the lesion in question could have been the site of a Burkitt's lymphoma. Wells (1964) and Sandison (1968, 1975), however, two noted authorities on paleopathology, expressed serious reservations about a malignant diagnosis, favoring the possibility of trauma and low-grade inflammation in causing formation of subperiosteal new bone. Sandison (1975) concluded that it is by no means proven that this lesion represents Burkitt's lymphoma or is even neoplastic.

Neolithic Period, Iron and Bronze Ages

Osteomata found in two femora from the Neolithic Period are clearly benign (Pales, 1930). However, an osteoid sarcoma was diagnosed in the right ulna of an adult man from the Neolithic Period found in Bassa Padana, Italy (Novello, 1981). A lesion in the neck of a humerus from West Kennet, Wiltshire, described as a possible neoplasm by Brothwell (1961), was later thought to be an abscess by Wells (1962). Several reports relate to possible myelomatosis in late Neolithic crania cited by Ackerknecht (1953) and from Norregard, Denmark (Brothwell and Sandison, 1967; 342) and the Pyrenees (Fusté, 1955), but insufficient description is given to render independent diagnosis. The Norregard skull, and an additional skull with lesions from Grossbremach, East Germany, are considered very improbable for cancer by one recent author (Soulie, 1980). The bone destruction of the Norregard skull may also be taken as evidence of postmortem bone erosion (Brothwell, 1967).

Soulie (1980) described a female skull, aged 50–70 years, from the European Bronze Age at Mokrin, Yugoslavia, showing perforated lesions. The inner table of bone shows clear traces of neovascularization. Two lesions are centered on the course of meningeal vessels. The author suggested neoplastic diffusion of carcinoma through the external carotid system. The malignant character of two lesions of a skull from the Grotte de Terrevaine at La Ciotat, Bouches du Rhone, was questioned based upon gross and radiographic observation (Soulie, 1980), in favor of pseudo-pathology caused by taphonomic transformation (see Chap. VI.)

"Carcinomatous" destruction of bone in the temporal area of a skull from a Winchester Saxon burial, and in the frontal area from an Iron Age skull from the Bernese Oberland, as well as "myelomatosis" in a medieval youth from Scarborough, England, have all been attributed to postmortem taphonomic changes (Brothwell, 1967). Insect destruction, as in the femur from a burial site on the Island of Socotra (Brothwell, 1963), may simulate neoplastic destruction of bone. Conversely, what has been described as postmortem soil erosion in an Iron Age skull from Switzerland by Hug (1959) may be a destructive tumor of the frontal sinuses (Brothwell, 1963). Hug (1956) has elsewhere described an osteosarcoma involving the left humeral head and extending along the proximal one-third of the shaft in another Swiss Iron Age skull from Munsingen. Postmortem erosion appears to have caused some irregularity in the appearance of the tumor (Brothwell, 1967). However, Jaffe (1958) points out that other tumors may simulate the appearance of osteosarcoma.

Ancient Egypt and Nubia

Ruffer (1921) examined hundreds of Egyptian mummies in the early part of the twentieth century. Many adult mummies in the over-50-year age group from Egypt have also been examined more recently (Sandison, 1970; Zimmerman, 1976). Extensive radiologic surveys of the large collections of mummies in European museums (Gray, 1967) and in the Cairo Museum (Harris and Weeks, 1973) have also been undertaken. Even so, meaningful occurrences of neoplasms in ancient Egypt have not been established (Sandison, 1980).

Initial diagnosis of an osteosarcoma in a femur from the cemetery of the Gizeh Pyramids (Fifth Dynasty) by Elliot Smith and Dawson (1924) has been more recently reinterpreted as a benign osteochondroma (Rowling, 1961). Likewise, Elliot Smith and Dawson (1924) refer to two cases of "sarcoma" in proximal humeri from Fifth Dynasty graves in Gizeh. However, no illustrations or morphologic descriptions are provided, and it is likely that these neoplasms may represent cases of mistaken diagnoses as well (Rowling, 1961; Brothwell, 1967). A pelvic tumor from an individual in the catacombs of Kom el-Shougafa in Alexandria, from Roman Egypt (A.D. 250–300) was originally described by Ruffer and

Willmore (1914) as an atypical osteosarcoma, but more likely represents a benign chondromatous process of long duration (Brothwell, 1967).

The relative lack of malignant epithelial tumors in ancient Egyptian mummies has been noted by Rowling (1961). Granville (1825) long ago described a large cyst of the right ovary and broad ligament in a Egyptian mummy, which may have represented a malignant cystadenocarcinoma of the ovary (Rowling, 1961) but is more likely a benign cystadenoma (Strouhal, 1975). In the relatively recent Byzantine Period, cases of malignant disease involving the nasopharynx and rectum, respectively, were suggested by Elliott-Smith and Dawson (1924) on the basis of destructive lesions in the base of the skull and sacrum. Wells (1963) also observed a primary lesion of a skull from the Third–Fifth Dynasty with twenty-six secondary deposits and destruction of the left maxillo-alveolar region which may represent carcinoma. Strouhal (1978) reported another case of nasopharyngeal carcinoma in a skull from the Fifth–Twelfth Dynasty in Upper Egypt. Derry (1909) described a similar case involving the cranial base of a pre-Christian Nubian (A.D. 300–500), and Elliott-Smith and Derry (1910) described a Middle Nubian male skeleton with erosion of the sacrum, possibly due to rectal cancer. However, these findings may also be the result of chordoma (Brothwell, 1967).

Changes in disease patterns were observed in ancient Nubia from 350 B.C. to A.D. 1400, with up to twelve malignant neoplasms reported for this later period (Armelagos, 1969). Marrocco and Armelagos also reported two malignant tumors in the remains of 223 individuals from a cemetary in lower Nubia dating from 350 B.C. to A.D. 500.

Among 222 skulls collected from a vast Coptic cemetery near El-Barsha from the early Christian period in Egypt (A.D. 400–600), five lesions were observed possibly consistent with nasal, oral and other carcinoma (El-Rokhawy et al., 1971).

Ancient Middle East

A skull from the Tepe Hessar site of Iran (3500–3000 B.C.) shows destruction of the left maxillary alveolus and antral wall and was cited by Krogman (1940) as an example of primary carcinoma.

Wada et al. (1987) described multiple lytic lesions in bones of a 25–30-year-old female from the Islamic period of Iraq. However, the relatively young age makes eosinophilic granuloma (Histiocytosis X) a diagnosis more likely than metastatic carcinoma or multiple myeloma (Steinbock, 1988).

The New World

Human populations in the New World may be considered "prehistoric," in a technical sense, prior to the arrival of Columbus five hundred years ago. For practical purposes, the search for cancer in antiquity may be limited to the pre-Columbian period in the New World, since the arrival of Columbus was associated with dramatic changes in life-style and marked the beginning of an evolution into disease patterns that are associated with the modern world.

MacCurdy (1923) attributed a tumor on a pre-Columbian skull from Peru to osteosarcoma. Brothwell (1967) reconsidered this tumor as a possible meningioma or angioma. Two cases of "myelomatosis" have also been reported in skeletal remains of an adult male (Ritchie and Warren 1932) and of a ten-year-old child (Williams, Ritchie and Titterington, 1941). It is more likely that the lesions of the child represent secondary neuroblastoma or another childhood disease (Brothwell, 1967). Hooton (1930) in 1930 recorded metastic tumor of vertebrae, right radius and ulna, and left radius in an Indian from Pecos Pueblo (early level). However, he did not describe the lesions in detail and provided no illustrations for comparative purposes. Steinbock (1976) re-examined this specimen in 1976 at the Peabody Museum and indicated that many of the skeletal findings are probably due to erosion and postmortem taphonomic transformation. Findings in a second skeleton cited by Hooton (1940) may also be explained on the basis of processes other than metastatic carcinoma (Steinbock, 1976). A pre-Columbian skull from a Peruvian collection was also reported to perhaps show evidence of metastatic carcinoma (Grana et al., 1954), although multiple trephinations also appear in the skulls of this collection (Brothwell, 1967).

In a survey of the mummies of Ica, Peru, representing five different pre-Columbian cultures dating from 600 B.C., no evidence of malignant neoplasms was found (Allison, Gertzen, Dalton, 1974). However, the same group of investigators recorded metastatic tumor in the skeleton of a female from the Tiahuanco Period of Chile (ca. A.D. 750) (Allison et al., 1980).

Two ancient Peruvians (before A.D. 1500) present evidence of metastatic carcinoma in the view of Steinbock (1976), a solitary skull from Llactashica and a skeleton from Huacho. The skeletons of several pre-Columbian mummies from Chancay, and Chongos, Ica, Peru, are felt to show evidence of malignant melanoma metastatic to bone (Urteaga and Pack, 1966).

In Canada, the earliest known human remains (at least 5500 years B.C.) show no evidence of primary or secondary bone tumors. During the archaic or equivalent cultural periods (1000–5500 years B.C.), two tumor-like bone conditions have been reported, one of which is a probable case of histiocytosis X in a child (Kennedy, 1983).

A Paleo-Eskimo skull (A.D. 400–1300), found in the Kitnepaluk necropolis in northwest St. Lawrence Island, Alaska, is reported to show evidence of malignant tumor or infection (Lagier et al., 1982). The skeleton of a prehistoric Eskimo from Kachemak Bay, Cook Inlet, Alaska, was also thought to show evidence of advanced malignant hemangioepithelioma (Lobdell, 1981). However, Gregg (1981) disagreed with this diagnosis for several reasons involving the epidemiology and pathology of this case. The findings could also be consistent with a benign process (Lobdell, 1981). Steinbock (1976) found evidence for metastatic carcinoma in two Alaskan Eskimo skulls (A.D. 500–1500) held in the Smithsonian Institution, and Cassidy (1977) observed a probable malignancy in the mandible of a Sadlermiut Eskimo from the historic period.

DOCUMENTARY EVIDENCE FOR CANCER IN ANTIQUITY

Zammit and Singer (1924) described two Neolithic human representations from Malta with artistic presentations of swelling in the abdomen and the groin. Two additional Neolithic figures from Sesklo, Greece, and Vinca, Yugoslavia, also show swelling in the region of the throat (Brothwell, 1967). The Neolithic art style was such (Zammit and Singer, 1924) that modern interpretations must remain tentative.

The Edwin Smith papyrus (approx. 1800 B.C.), Ebers papyrus (approx. 1550 B.C.) and Kahun papyrus (approx. 1750 B.C.) are representative of Egyptian medical papyri. Early translations of these Egyptian texts were lacking both in terms of Egyptology (Dawson, 1953) and medical history (Ghalioungui, 1963). In light of their contents, the Ebers is thought of as a medical text, the Edwin Smith surgical and the Kahun gynecological. The Ebers papyrus has a series of prescriptions, believed to be the remains of a "book on tumors," which deals with tumors and swellings (Ghalioungui, 1963). These tumors appear to have consisted of benign ganglionic masses, polyps, sebaceous cysts, varicose veins and aneurysms.

There is a reference to the "tumors of Chon" in which Brothwell (1967) finds possible evidence of malignancy, but which Ghaliongui (1963) cites as a "model clinical description" of leprosy. Elsewhere, "tumors of Chon" were originally translated as tubercular leprosy, but Ghalioungui (1963) feels that the description better represents gas gangrene or possibly cancer. Esmond R. Long in *A History of Pathology* (1928) describes "ulcerating lumps" in the Ebers and Edwin Smith papyri "that might be construed as cancer." In this case, the interpretation was more conservative than in some of those that followed. The word "tumor" appears frequently but always in the sense of swelling. The legendary rumor that malignant melanoma was described in the Ebers papyrus is apparently apocryphal (Urteaga and Pack, 1966).

Long (1928) also recounts Herodotus's story (III:33) that Democedes of Crotona (520 B.C.), founder of the medical school in Athens, healed the Persian Darius's wife Athossa (daughter of Cyrus the Great) of a cancer of the breast. However, the disease appears to actually have been inflammatory mastitis (Sandison, 1959; Brothwell, 1967).

The Greek Dioscorides in the first century A.D. employed a drug made from autumn crocus (*Colchicum autumnale* L.) and wrote that "the plant (*Kolchikon*) should be soaked in wine and administered to dissolve tumors (*oidemata*) and growths (*phumata*) not yet making pus" (Riddle, 1985). Dioscorides's terms *oidemata* and *phumutu* may have included malignancies, but their use clearly was not restricted to malignant conditions. Galen (A.D. 129–210) and the Byzantine physicians used the term *onkos* to cover all types of swellings, tumors and lesions. Galen's Greek term *Karkinos* (or *karkinoma;* Latin, *cancer*) could not have exclusively been applied to malignancies.

In ancient India, medical conditions were described in the Rigveda (3000 B.C.), Ayurveda, Ramayana and other texts. A few human remains from prehistoric India and the Indus River Valley civilization have been unearthed at Harappa in Punjab, Lothul in Gujarut and Inamgoen in Maharashtra. However, the state of decomposition precludes any assessment of health status (Suraiya, 1973), and the writings in the ancient texts cannot be verified against material remains.

Neck tumors mentioned in the Vedas are probably endemic goiter, as commonly encountered in some highland Aryan tribes living in the Himalayas, although a fatal tumor of the throat is described in the Atharvaveda (Suraiya, 1973). The physician Sushruta (approx. 600 B.C.) compiled a surgical treatise in which a chapter is devoted to *arbuda*, glands and tumors. Here *arbuda* is a swelling with characteristics that may implicate a malignant process. Overindulgence in eating meat is listed as one of the causes of *arbuda*. One description of *arbuda* is consistent with ulceration.

Tumors arising from other specific sites are not treated in the chapter on *arbuda* but described separately under different names. The practice of chewing betel nut is very ancient in India, and Sushruta describes cancers of the lip, alveolus, tongue, palate and pharynx, manifesting "lotus-like" growths. Tumors described in the post-cricoidal gastrointestinal tract appear benign. Approximately twenty diseases of the female breast and genital organs are described, but none are consistent with cancer of the uterus, ovaries or breast. Part of the criteria used to assign a described disease to the category of malignancy is whether the disease is considered by the ancient author to be fatal (Suraiya, 1973). However, we must keep in mind that not all fatal diseases associated with swellings were cancers in the pre-antibiotic era.

CANCER IN MODERN SOCIETIES

Modern primate populations and contemporary societies around the world that follow a traditional life-style may also provide insights into the origins of human cancer. No cancer was observed among diseases of wild apes (Schultz, 1967), for example. Several diseases are also characteristically uncommon among populations following a traditional life-style, including myocardial infarction and carcinoma of the lung (Polunin, 1967). Adenocarcinoma (glandular cancer) involving breast, colon, pancreas or prostate also appears to be rare in traditional societies (Micozzi, 1985).

On the other hand, as reliable modern data were collected, it was recognized that oral and nasopharyngeal cancers are relatively common in parts of Africa (Clifford, 1961) and China (Kaplan and Jones, 1978). These patterns in contemporary Asian and African populations may be related to evidence for oral and nasopharyngeal cancers in Ancient Egypt and India as documented in human remains and medical texts. However, ancient evidence for the modern so-called "cancers of civilization" (Micozzi, 1985) remains elusive or simply nonexistent in examinations conducted around the world over the past century. Understanding postmortem transformation of human and animal remains is important in interpreting the case for cancer in antiquity.

REFERENCES

Abel, O. 1924. "Nuere Studien uber Krankheiten fossiler Wirbeltiere." *Verhandl. d. zool. botan. ges. Wien* 73: 104.

Adelson, Lester. 1974. *The Pathology of Homicide: A Vade Mecum Counsel.* Springfield: Charles C Thomas.

Alexander, A. 1956. "Bone carrying by Porcupines." *South African Journal of Science* 52: 257–258.

Allison, M.J., Gerszten, E., Dalton, H.P. 1974. "Paleopathology in Pre-Columbian Americans." *Lab. Invest.* 30: 407–408.

Allison, M.J., Gerszten, E., Munizaga, J., Santoro, C. 1980. "Metastatic tumor of bone in a Tiahuanaco female." *Bull. NY. Acad. Med.* 56: 581–587.

Allman, T.D. 1981. "Credit cards and calculators come to Shangri-La." *Asia* 3 (5): 26–44.

Aries, Philippe. 1974. *Western Attitudes toward Death: From the Middle Ages to the Present.* Baltimore: Johns Hopkins Press.

Armelagos, G.J. 1969. "Disease in ancient Nubia: Changes in disease patterns from 350 B.C. to A.D. 1400 demonstrate the interaction of biology and culture." *Science* 163: 255–259.

Armelagos, G.A. 1980. *Science* 209. 1532–1534.

Arnaud, G., Arnaud, S., Baud, C. and Lagier, R. 1980. "Histological study of buried, sea-immersed and lake-immersed bones." *Paleopathology Newsletter.* Papers on Paleopathology. Third European Meeting of the Paleopathology Association, Caen, France. p. C2.

Artamonov, M.L. 1965. "Frozen tombs of the Scythians." *Scientific American* 212 (5): 101–109.

Ascher, R. 1968. "Time's Arrow and the Archeology of a Contemporary Community." In *Settlement Archaeology,* edited by K.C. Chang. Palo Alto, CA: National Press.

Attwell, R.I.G. 1963. "Some observations on feeding habits, behavior and inter-relationships of Rhodesian vultures." *Ostrich* 34: 235–247.

Aufderheide, A.C. 1980. "Soft Tissue Anatomic Findings in Three Basket-Maker Mummies." *Abstracts: Annual Meeting of the Paleopathology Association,* p. NF 4, Niagara Falls, New York.

——. 1981. "Soft tissue Paleopathology—an emerging subspeciality." *Human Pathology* 12: 865–867.

——. 1983. "Alkaptonuria: Work in progress." *Paleopathology Newsletter* 43: 7.

Baden, Michael M. 1982. "Medical-Legal Aspects of Microbiology." *New York Academy of Sciences,* Section of Microbiology, February 17.

Bass, W.B. 1984. Time interval since death: A difficult decision. In Rathbun, T.A. and Buikstra, J.E. (eds.) *Human Identification: Case Studies in Forensic Anthropology,* Springfield, IL.; Charles C Thomas, pp. 136–147.

Behrensmeyher, A.K. 1975a. "The Taphonomy and Paleoecology of Plio-Pleistocene Vertebrate Assemblages East of Lake Rudolf, Kenya." *Bulletin of the Museum of Comparative Zoology 196:* 473–578.

――――. 1975b. "Taphonomy and Paleoecology in the Hominid Fossil Record." In *Yearbook of Physical Anthropology* 19, Edited by J. Buetner-Janush, p. 36–50.

――――. 1978. "Taphonomic and Ecologic Information from Bone Weathering." *Paleobiology* 4 (2): 150–162.

Bergeret, M. 1850. Infanticide, momification du cadavre. decouverte du cadavre d'un enfant nouveau-ne' duns une cheminee ou il s'etait momifie. Determination de l'epoque de la naissance par la presence de nymphes et de larves d' insectes dans le cadavre et par l'etude de leurs metamorphoses. *Ann. Hyg. Med. Leg* 4: 442–52.

Binford, Lewis R. 1977. General Introduction. In *For Theory Building in Archaeology,* edited by L.R. Binford, New York: Academic Press, p. 1–10.

――――. 1978a. "Dimensional analysis of behavior and site structure: learning from an Eskimo hunting stand." *American Antiquity* 43: 330–361.

――――. 1978b. *Nunamiut Ethnoarchaeology.* New York: Academic Press.

――――. 1979. "Comments on confusion." *American Antiquity* 44: 591–594.

――――. 1980. "Willow smoke and dog tails: Hunter-Gatherer settlement systems and archaeologic site formation." *American Antiquity* 45: 4–20.

――――. 1981b. *Bones: Ancient Men and Modern Myths.* New York: Academic Press.

Binford, L.R., and J.B. Bertram. 1977. "Bone Frequencies and Attritional Processes." *For Theory Building in Archaeology,* edited by L.R. Binford. New York: Academic Press. pp. 77–153.

Birket-Smith, L. 1957. *Primitive Man and His Ways.* Cleveland: World Publishing.

Bjeldanes, L.F. and G.W. Chang. 1977. "Mint plant component, flavonoid toxicity suggested." *Food Chemical News* 19 (21): 32.

Blair, L. and Blair, L. 1988. *Ring of Fire: Exploring the Last Remote Places of the World.* Toronto: Bantam.

Boaz, N.T., and A.K. Behrensmeyer. 1976. "Hominid taphonomy: transport of human skeletal parts in an artificial fluviate environment." *Am. J. Phy. Anthro.* 45: 53–60.

Bordaz, J., and V. Bordaz. 1966. "A critical examination of data processing, with an evaluation of a new inverted data system." *American Antiquity* 31: 494–501.

Bourque, J., and K. Morris. 1978. "Determining the season of death of mammal teeth from archaeologic sites: a new sectioning technique." *Science* 199: 530–531.

Bourliere, F. 1963. "Specific feeding habits of African carnivores." *African Wild Life* 17: (1) 21–27.

――――. 1966. "Observations on the Ecology of Some Large African Mammals." In *African Ecology and Human Evolution,* edited by F.C. Howell and F. Bourliere, Chicago: Aldine, pp. 43–54.

Brain, C.K. 1969. "The Contribution of Namib Desert Hottentots to an Understanding of Australopithecine Bone Accumulations." Scientific Papers of the Namib Desert Research Station 13.

———. 1980. "Some Criteria for Recognition of Bone-Collecting Agencies in African Caves." In *Fossils in the Making: Vertebrate Taphonomy and Paleoecology*, edited by A.K. Behrensmeyer and A.P. Hill. pp. 107–130.

———. 1981. *The Hunters or the Hunted? An Introduction to African Cave Taphonomy.* Chicago: University of Chicago Press.

Brannon, C.H. 1934. "Observations on the blow-fly, *lucilia sericata meig.*" *Journal Parasitology* 20: 190–194.

Brothwell, D. 1967. *The Evidence for Neoplasms.* pp. 320–345 in Brothwell and Sandison.

Brothwell, D., Sandison, A.T. (eds.). 1967. *Diseases in Antiquity: A Survey of the Diseases, Injuries and Surgery of Early Populations.* Springfield, IL; Charles C Thomas, 766 pages.

Brothwell, D.R., Sandison, A.T., Gray, D.H.R. 1969. "Human biological observations on Guanche mummy with anthracosis." *Am. J. Phy. Anthro* 30: 333–347.

Brothwell, D.R. 1963. *Digging Up Bones.* London; British Museum (Natural History).

Budge, E.A.T.W. 1925. *The Mummy: A Handbook of Egyptian Funerary Archaeology,* Cambridge: Cambridge University Press, p. 290.

Butterfield, W.C. 1966. "Tumor treatment, 3000 B.C." *Surgery* 60: 479–9.

Calder, W.A. 1984. *Size, Function and Life History.* Cambridge, MA; Harvard University Press.

Carpenter, H.M., Wilkins, R.M. 1964. "Autopsy bacteriology: review of 2,033 cases. *Arch. Pathol.* 77: 73–79.

Cassidy, C.M. 1977. "Probable malignancy in a Sadlermiut Eskimo mandible." *Am. J. Phys. Anthro.* 46: 291–296.

Castiglioni, A. (author of original monograph in Italian), Krumbhaar, E.B. (translator and editor of English edition). *A History of Medicine,* see relevent passages on pp. 163–164, 252–255, 676–677, 798–800, 843–853, 1016–1017, 1072–1074, and 1099–1101.

Cavallite, C.J., Buck, J.S., Suter, L.M. 1944. "Allicin, the antibacterial principle of allium sativum." *Journal of the American Chemical Society* 66: 1952.

Chaplin, R.E. 1969. "The Use of Non-Morphological Criteria in the Study of Animal Domestication from Bones Found in Archaeologic Sites." *In The Domestication of Plants and Animals,* edited by P.J. Ucko and G.W. Dimbleby, Chicago: Aldine. pp. 231–245.

Childe, V. Gordon. 1956. *Piecing Together the Past.* New York; Praeger. London; Routledge and Kegan, Paul.

Clark, J.D. 1960. "Human ecology during the Pleistocene and later times in Africa south of the Sahara." *Current Anthropology* 1: 307–324.

Clausen, C.J., Cohen, A.D., Emiliani, C., Holman, J.A., Stipp, J.J. 1979. "Little Salt Spring, Florida: a unique underwater site." *Science* 203: 6.

Clifford, P. 1961. "Malignant disease of the nose, paranasal sinuses and post-nasal space in East Africa." *J. Laryngology and Otology* 75: 707–733.

Cockburn, A., Cockburn, E. (eds.). 1980. *Mummies, Disease and Ancient Cultures* [abridged edition.]. Cambridge Univ. Press, Cambridge; 234 pages.

Coley, B.L. 1960. *Neoplasms of Bone.* New York; Hoeber, pp. 8–13.

Contributions to North American Ethnology. 1887. Vol. I.

Cornaby, B.W. 1974. "Carrion reduction by animals in contrasting tropical habitats, *Biotropica* 6: 51–63.

Cotton, G. Aufderheide, A.C., Goldschmidt, V. G. 1987. "Preservation of human tissue immersed for five years in fresh water of known temperature." *Journal of Forensic Sciences* 32: 1125–1130.

Coughlin, E.A. 1977. "The Effects of botanical products on rehydrated mummified tissue and on experimentally mummified tissue." *Paleopathology Newsletter.* 17: 7–8.

Couzis, K. 1903. *"Die Krebskranheit bei den griechischen Aerzten des Altertums,"* Athens; [Reviewed by Gavalas, S.A.].

Crader, D.C. 1974. "The effects of scavengers on the bone material from a large mammal: an experiment conducted among the Bisa of the Luanga Valley, Zambia." In *Ethnoarchaeology,* edited by B.C. Connan and C.W. Clewlow, Mono. 4. Los Angeles: Institute of Archaeology, University of California. pp. 161–173.

Currey, J.D. 1968. The effect of protection on the impact strength of rabbit bones. *Acta Anat.* 71: 87–93.

Cybulski, J. S. 1978. "Modified human bones and skulls from Prince Rupert Harbour, British Columbia." *Canadian Journal of Archaeology* 2: 15–32.

Cybulski, J.S., Pett, L.B. "Bone changes suggesting multiple myeloma and metastatic carcinoma in two early historic natives of the British Columbia coast." In Cybulski, J.S. (ed.), *Contributions to Physical Anthropology 1978–1980,* Nat. Mus. of Man Mercury Series, Arch. Survey of Canada paper No. 106. Nat. Mus. of Canada, Ottawa, 1981.

Dall, W.H. 1878. "On the remains of later prehistoric man." *Smithsonian Contribution to Knowledge,* Vol. 22.

Daly, P. 1969. "Approaches to faunal analysis in archaeology." *American Antiquity* 34: 146–153.

Daniels, F., and Post, P.W. 1970. "The Histology and Histochemistry of Prehistoric Mummy Skin." In *Adv. in Biology of Skin,* Vol. X: The Dermis, W. Montagno, J.P. Bently, R.L. Dobson. pp. 279–292. New York: Appleton-Century-Crofts.

Dart, Raymond. 1957. "The Osteodontokeratic Culture of Australopithecus Prometheus." *Transvasal Museum Memoir* 18.

Darwin, Charles. 1896. *Formation of Vegetable Mould through the Action of Worms.* New York: Appleton.

Dastugue, J. 1980. "Possibilities, limits and prospects in paleopathology of the human skeleton." *J. Human Evolution* 9: 3–8.

Dawson, W.R. 1927. "Contributions to the History of Mummification." *Proc. Royal Society of Medicine,* 832–854.

Dawson, W.R. 1953. The Egyptian Medical Papyri. In Underwood EA (ed), *Science, Medicine and History.* Oxford Univ. Press, London.

——. 1934. *Journal of Egyptian Archaeology* 20: 170.

Decker, P. 1978. "Post-mortem bacteriology." *Bulletin of the Ayer Clinical Laboratory,* New Series 4 (2): 2–5.

Derry, D.E. 1909. Anatomical Report. *Arch. Survey Nubia Bull* 3: 29–52.

Dodson, Peter. 1973. "The Significance of Small Bones in Paleoecological Interpretations." *University of Wyoming Contributions to Geology* 12: 15–19.

Dolan, C.T., Brown, A.L., Ritts, R.E. 1971. "Microbiological examination of postmortem tissues." *Arch. Path.* 92: 206–211.

Dowd, J.T. 1980. "The investigation of the vandalized graves of two historic personages: Osceola, Seminole war chief, and Colonel William M. Shy, Civil War Hero." *Tennessee Anthropologist* 5: 47–72.

Duffield, L.F. 1970. "Vertisols and their implications in archaeological research." *American Anthropologist* 72: 1055–1062.

Early, M., Goff, M.L. 1986. "Arthropod succession patterns in exposed carrion on the island of Oahu, Hawaiian Islands, U.S.A., *J. Med. Entomol.* 23: 520–31.

Efremov, I.A. 1940. "Taphonomy: a new branch of paleontology." *Pan-American Geologist* 74: 81–93.

Elkin, A.P. 1953. *The Australian Aborigines.* Sydney: Angus and Robertson.

Elliot Smith, G. 1909. Anatomical report. *Arch. Survey Nubia Bull* 4: 19–21.

Elliot Smith, G., Dawson, W.R. 1924. *Egyptian Mummies.* Dial Press, New York, [also Allen and Unwin, London, 1924].

Elliot Smith, G., Dawson, W.R. 1924. *"Mummification in Relation to Medicine and Pathology."* Chap. X, pages 154–162, in Elliot Smith and Dawson.

Elliot Smith, G., Derry, D.E. 1910. "Anatomical report." *Arch. Survey Nubia Bull* 5: 11–25.

Elliot Smith, G., Wood Jones, F. 1908. Anatomical report. *Arch. Survey Nubia Bull* 3: 29–54.

El-Najjar, M.Y. McWilliams, K.R. 1978. *Forensic Anthropology,* Springfield, IL; Charles C Thomas.

El-Najjar, M.Y., Mulinski, T.M.J. 1980. "Mummies and Mummification Practices in the Southwestern and Southern United States." In Cockburn, A. and Cockburn, E., *Mummies, Disease and Ancient Cultures,* Cambridge; Cambridge University Press, pp. 103–110.

El-Rakhawy, M.T., El-Eishi, H.I., El-Nofely A., Gaballah M. F. 1971. "A contribution to pathology of ancient Egyptian skulls." *Anthropologie* 9: 71–78.

Engelbach, R. and Derry, D. 1942. "Mummification." *Annales du Service des Antiquites de l'Egypte* 41: 236–238.

Esper, E.J.C. Ausfuhrliche nachrichten von neuendeckten zoolithen unbekannter vierfussiger Thiere. Nurnberg, 1774.

Evans, W.E.D. 1963a. *The Chemistry of Death.* Ch. 7, Springfield, IL: Charles C Thomas.

———. 1963b. "Adipocere formation in a relatively dry environment." *Med. Sci. Law* 3: 145–153.

Farrow, J.H. 1971. "Antiquity of breast cancer." *Cancer* 28: 1369–1371.

Fawkes, J.C. 1914. *Smithsonian Miscellaneous Collections.* No. 63.

Feldman, E. 1977. "Biblical and post-biblical defilements and mourning. *Law and Theology.*" New York: Yeshiva University Press.

Flinn, L., Turner, C.G., Brew, A. 1976. "Additional evidence for cannibalism in the Southwest." *American Antiquity* 41: 308–318.

Fredickson, A.G., Stephonopoulos, G. 1981. "Microbial competition." *Science* 213: 972–979.

Fuller, M.E. 1934. "The insect inhabitants of carrion: a study in animal ecology." *Australian C.S.I.R.O. Bulletin* 82: 5–62.

Galloway, A., Birkby, W.H., Jones, A.M., Henry, T.E., Parks, B.O. 1989. "Decay rates of human remains in an arid environment." *J. Forensic Sci.* 34: 617–621.

Garrison, F.H. 1914. *"An Introduction to the History of Medicine – with Medical Chronology, Bibliographic Data and Test Questions."* Saunders, Philadelphia; 1214 pages.

Ghalioungui, P. 1963. *Magic and Medical Science in Ancient Egypt.* Hodder & Stoughton, London, England; pp. 84–91.

Giacometti, L., Chiarelli, B. 1968. "The skin of Egyptian mummies: a study in survival." *Arch. Dermatol* 97: 712–716.

Gifford, Diane P. 1978. "Ethnoarchaeological Observations of Natural Processes Affecting Cultural Materials." In *Explorations in Ethnoarchaeology,* edited by R.J. Gould, pp. 77–101. Albuquerque: University of New Mexico Press.

——. 1981. "Taphonomy and Paleoecology: A Critical Review of Archaeology's Sister Discipline." In *Advances in Archaeological Method and Theory.* Vol. 4, ed. M.B. Schiffer, pp. 365–438. New York: Academic Press.

Gillman, H. 1875. "Certain characteristics pertaining to ancient man in Michigan." Annual Report of the Smithsonian Institution for 1875, pp. 234–245, Washington, D.C.

Glob, P.V. 1969. *The Bog People.* New York: Cornell University Press.

Goff, M.L., Omori, A.I., Gunatilake 1988. "Estimation of post-mortem interval by arthropod succession: three case studies from the Hawaiian Islands." *Am. J. Forensic Med. Pathol.* 9: 220–225.

Goldfuss, A. 1810. "Die umegebungen von Muggendorf." *Erlanger:* 276.

Goldstein, M.S. 1969. In Brothwell, D., Higgs, E., *Science and Archaeology,* London.

Goodman, M., Barnhart, M.I., Shoshani, J., Romero-Herrera, A.E. 1980. "Molecular Studies on the Magadan Mammoth." *Abstracts: Annual Meeting of the Paleopathology Association,* p. NF 4. Niagara Falls, New York.

Gould, R.A. 1978. "The anthropology of human residues." *American Anthropologist* 80: 815–834.

Grady, P.H.K. 1967. "Radiography of ancient Egyptian mummies." *Med Radiogr. Photogr.* 43: 34–44.

Graham-Smith, G.S. 1916. "Observations on the habits and parasites of common flies." *Parasitology* 8: 440–546.

Grana, F., Rocca, E.D., Grana, L. 1954. Las Trepanaciones Craneanas en el Peru en la Epoca pre-Hispanica. Lima: Maria.

Granville, A.B. 1825. "An essay on Egyptian Mummies with observations on the art of embalming among the ancient Egyptians." XIII. *Philosophical Transactions* 115: 269–316.

Gregg, J.B. 1981. Annotated bibliography. *Paleopathology Newsletter:* 15–16.

Grollman, A. 1974. *Concerning Death: A Practical Guide for the Living.* Boston: Beacon Press.

Guernsey, S.J., Kidder, A.V. 1919. "Basket Maker caves of Northeastern Arizona." *Papers of Peabody Museum on American Archaeology.* VIII. No. 2.

Guthe, Carl E. 1937. "A burial site on the Island of Samar, Philippines." *Papers of the Michigan Academy of Science, Arts and Letters* Vol. XIII.

Guaman Poma de Ayala, F. 1956. Nueva Coronica y Buen Gobierno [ca. 1613] L.F. Bustios Galvez (ed.) Lima.

Haglund, W.D., Reay, D.T., Swindler, D.R. 1988. "Tooth mark artifacts and survival of bones in animal scavenged human skeletons." *J Forensic Sci.* 33: 985–997.

Haglund, W.D., Reay, D.T., Swindler, D.R. 1989. "Canid scavenging disarticulation sequence of human remains in the Pacific Northwest. *J. Forensic Sci.* 34: 587–606.

Hamlyn Harris, R. 1913. "Mummification in Papua." *American Anthropologist, New Series* Vol. XV. Lancaster.

Hanson, C.B. 1980. "Fluvial Taphonomic Processes: Models and Requirements." In *Behrensmeyer and Hill.*

Hanson, D.B., Buikstra, J.E. 1987. "Histomorphological alterations in buried human bodies from the Lower Illinois Valley: Implications for paleodietary research." *J. Archaeol. Research* 14: 549–563.

Harris, J.E., Weeks, K.R. 1973. *X-Raying the Pharoahs.* New York: Charles Scribners.

Hart, G.D. (ed). 1983. *Disease in Ancient Man.* Clarke Irwin, Agincourt, Ontario.

Haskell, N.H., McShaffrey, D.G., Hawley, D.A., Williams, R.E., Pless, J.E. 1989. "Use of acquatic insects in determining submersion interval." *J. Forensic Sci.* 34: 622–632.

Hawley, D.A., Haskell, N.H., McShaffray, D.G., Williams, R.E., Pless, J.E. 1989. "Identification of a red "fiber": Chironomid larvae." *J. Forensic Sci.* 34: 617–621.

Herodotus. *The Histories,* translated by Aubrey de Selincourt. London and Baltimore: Penguin Classics.

Hill, A.P. 1977. "Disarticulation and scattering of mammal skeletons." *Paleobiology* 5: 261–274.

———. 1979. "Butchering and natural disarticulation: an investigatory technique." *American Antiquity* 44: 739–744.

Hongi, H. 1916. *Journal of Polynesian Society,* Vol. XXV.

Hooton, E.A. 1940 "The Indians of Pecos Pueblo. A study of their skeletal remains." *New Haven:* Yale Univ. Press.

Hope, F.W. 1834. "Notice of several species of insects found in the heads of Egyptian mummies." *Transactions of the Entomological Society of London* (Proceedings). 1: xi–xiii.

Horne, Patrick. 1980. "The Death of Charles Francis Hall, Arctic Explorer." *Abstracts: Annual Meeting of the Paleopathology Association,* p. NF 2, Niagara Falls, New York.

Howell, F.C. 1961. "Ismilia: A paleolithic site in Africa" *Scientific American* 205 (4): 118–129.

Hrdlicka, A. 1905. *The Painting of Human Bones Among the American Aborignes.* Annual report of the Smithsonian Institution for 1904, pp. 607–617. Washington, D.C.

Hug, E. 1956. *Die Anthropologische Sammlung in Naturhistorischen Museum, Bern.* Bern, Switzerland, Natural History Museum.

Hug, E. 1959. *Die Anthropologische Sammlung in Kantonsmuseum Baselland.* Liestal, Kantonsmuseum Baselland.

Hughes, A.R. 1954. "Hyenas vs Australopithecines as agents of bone accumulation." *Am. J. Phys. Anthro.* 12: 467–486.

Issac, G.C. 1967. "Toward the Interpretation of Occupation Debris: Some Experiments and Observations." *Kroeber Anthro. Society Papers* 37: 31–57.

Jaffe, H.L. 1958. *Tumors and Tumorous Conditions of the Bones and Joints:* London; Kimpton.

Jambor, J. 1988. "Changes in bones of prehistoric population caused by environmental influence." *Anthropology* 26: 55–60.

James, E.O. 1957. *Prehistoric Religion.* New York: Praeger.

Jansen, H.W. 1971. *History of Art.* Englewood Cliffs, N.J.: Prentice-Hall.

Jiron, L.F., Cartin, V.M. "Insect succession in the decomposition of a mammal in Costa Rica." *J. New York Entomol. Soc.* 89: 158–165.

Johnson, D. 1975. "Seasonal and microseral variation in the insect population on carrion." *American Midland Naturalist* 93 (1): 79–90.

de Jongh, D.S., Leftis, J.W., Green, J.S., Shively, J.A., Minckler, T.M. 1968. "Postmortem bacteriology: a practical method for routine use." *American J. Clinical Pathology* 49: 424–428.

Kaplan, H.S., Jones, P. 1978. *Cancer in China.* New York: A.R. Liss, 236 pp.

Kelley, M.A., El-Najjar, M.Y. 1980. Natural variations and diferential diagnosis of skeletal changes in tuberculosis. *Am. J. Phys. Anthro.* 52: 153–167.

Kelley, M.A., Micozzi, M.S. 1984. Rib lesions in chronic pulmonary tuberculosis. *Am. J. Phys. Anthro.* 65: 381–386.

Klein, R.G. 1980. *The interpretation of mammalian fauna from stone age archaeological sites with special reference to sites in the Southern Cape Province, South Africa.* In *Behrensmeyer and Hill,* pp. 223–246.

Knapp, E.E., Kent, T.H. 1968. "Post-mortem lung cultures." *Arch. Path.* 85: 200–203.

Koneman, E.W., Davis, M.A. 1974. "Post-mortem bacteriology. III. clinical significance of microorganisms recovered at autopsy." *Am. J. Clin. Path.* 55: 17–23.

Koneman, E.W., Minckler, T.M. Shires, D.B., de Jongh, D.S. 1971. "Post-mortem bacteriology II. Selection of cases for culture." *Am. J. Clin. Pathol.* 55: 17–23.

Kopytoff, Igor. 1971. "Ancestors as Elders in Africa." *Africa* 41: 129–142.

Krogman, W.M. 1962. *The Human Skeleton in Forensic Medicine,* Springfield, IL; Charles C Thomas.

——. 1940. "The skeletal and dental pathology of an early Iranian site." *Bull Hist. Med.* 8: 28.

Krogman, W.M., Iscan, M.Y. 1985. *The Human Skeleton in Forensic Medicine,* Springfield, IL; Charles C Thomas.

Krook, J. 1969. "Man's early challenge to neoplasms." *Minnesota Med.* 52: 1159–1164.

Kruuk, H. 1970. "Interactions between Populations of Spotted Hyena (*Crocuta crocuta erxben*) and Their Prey Species." In *Animal Populations in Relation to Their Food Resources,* ed. A. Watson. Oxford: Blackwell. pp. 359–374.

———. 1972a. *The Spotted Hyena: A Study of Predation and Social Behavior.* Chicago: University of Chicago Press.

———. 1972b. "Competition for food between vultures in East Africa." *Ardea* 55: 171–193.

Lagier, R., Baud, C.A., Arnaud, G., Arnaud, S., Menk, R. 1982. "Lesions characteristic of infection or malignant tumor in paleo-eskimo skulls." *Virchows Arch.* [Pathol. Anat.] 395: 237–243.

Lantis, M. 1971. *Alaskan Eskimo Ceremonialism.* Seattle: University of Washington Press.

Lawrence, D.R. 1968. "Taphonomy and information losses in fossil communities." *Geological Society of America Bulletin* 79: 1315–1330.

Lawrence, J.E.P. 1935. Appendix A, in Leakey, L.S., *Stone Age Races of Kenya.* Oxford University, London: 139.

Lehrer, R.I., Howard, D.H., Sypherd, P.S., *et al.* 1980. "Mucormycosis." *Annals of Internal Medicine* Vol. 93, pp. 93–108.

Lipmann, M.E., Lichter, A.S., Danforth, D.N. 1988. *Diagnosis and Management of Breast Cancer.* Philadelphia; Saunders, pp. 96–99.

Lips, J.E. 1947. *The Origin of Things.* New York: A. A. Wyn

Lobdell, J.E. "The occurrence of a rare cancer in a prehistoric Eskimo skeleton from Kachemak Bay, Cook Inlet, Alaska." In Cybulski, J.S. (ed), *Contributions to Physical Anthropology* 1978–1980. Nat. Mus. of Man Mercury Series, Arch. Survey of Canada paper No. 106. Nat. Mus. of Canada, Ottawa, 1981.

Long, E.R. 1928. *A History of Pathology.* Baltimore; Williams & Wilkins, 291 pages.

Lucas, A. 1932. "The use of natron in mummification." *Journal of Egyptian Archaeology* 18: 125–140.

Lucas, A., Harris, J. 1962. "Mummification." In *Ancient Egyptian Materials and Industries.* London: Arnold. pp. 270–326.

Lull, R.S. 1933. "A revision of the Ceratopsia." *Memoirs of the Peabody Museum of Natural History,* III, Part 3, p. 131 and Fig. 42., *New Haven.*

Lyell, C. 1867. *Principles of Geology.* London. 2 vols, 10th ed.

Lyon, P.J. 1970. "Differential bone destruction: an ethnographic example." *American Antiquity* 35: 213–215.

Macalister, R.A.S. 1921. *A Textbook of European Archaeology.* Cambridge: Cambridge University Press.

MacCurdy, G.G. 1923. "Human skeletal remains from the highlands of Peru." *Am. J. Phys. Anthro.* 6: 217.

Malefijt, A. 1969. *Religion and Culture.* New York: MacMillan.

Mant, A.K. and R. Furbank. 1957. "Adipocere—a review." *J. Forensic Medicine* 4: 18–35.

Marchiafava, V., Bonucci, E., Ascenzi, A. 1974. "Fungal osteoclasia: a model of dead bone resorption." *Calcif. Tissue Res.* 14: 195–210.

Marrocco, G.R., Armelagos, G.J. 1984. *Tumors in a Nubian Population. Symposium on Tumors in Antiquity.* Paleopathology Association. Paleopathology Newsletter, p. 1–3.

Mayer, D.R. 1854. "Uber krankhafter knochen vorweltlicher thiere." *Nova Acta*

Leopoldina [Novorum Actorum Academia Caesareae Leopoldino—Carolinae Naturae (uriosum)], Bd. xxiv, part ii; pp. 673–689, Plate 30.

McConnel, V. 1957. *Myths of the Mun Kan.* Melbourne: Melbourne University Press.

McCullough, O.R. 1970. "Secondary Productions of Birds and Mammals." In *Analysis of Temperate Forest Ecosystems,* edited by D. E. Reichle. Ecological Studies, Vol. I. Heidelberg, pp. 107–130.

McHargue, G. 1972. *Mummies.* New York: MacMillan.

Megnin, J.P. 1887. La Fauna des tombeaux. C.R. Acad. Sci Paris. 105: 948–951.

Megnin, J.P. 1894. "La Fauna des Cadavres. Application de L'entomologie a la Medicine Legale." *Encyclopedie Scientifique des Aide-memoires,* Paris, Masson, p. 214.

Merch, C.H. 1937. *Ethnographische Beobachtunger uber die Volker des Beringsmeers 1789-1791.* Baess. Archives.

Mettler, C.C., Mettler, F.A. 1947. *History of Medicine.* Blakiston: Philadelphia; pp. 240–243, 813, 920–923.

Micozzi, M.S. 1986. "Experimental study of postmortem change under field conditions: effects of freezing, thawing and mechanical injury. *Journal of Forensic Sciences* 31 (3): 953–961.

Micozzi, M.S. 1985. Nutrition, body size and breast cancer. *Yearbook of Physical Anthropology* 28: 175–206.

Micozzi, M.S. 1982. Skeletal tuberculosis, pelvic contraction and parturition. *Am. J. Phys. Anthropology.* 58: 441–445.

Miller, J.A. 1979. "Chemistry: Spicing up a Peppery Issue," and "Into Onions: Tears and Therapies." *Science News* 115 (16): 265.

Milner, G.R., Smith, V.G. 1989. "Carnivore alterations of human bone from a prehistoric site in Illinois." *Am. J. Phys. Anthro.* 79: 43–49.

Minckler, T.M., Nowell, G.R., O'Toole, W.F., Niwayama, G., Levine, P.H. 1966. "Microbiology experience in the collection of human tissue." *American J. of Clinical Pathology* 45: 85–92.

Moodie, R.L. "General considerations of the evidences of pathological conditions found among fossil animals"; pp. 31–46 in Brothwell and Sandison, 1967. [Condensed and edited from Moodie, R.L., *Ann Med. His.* 1, 1917: 374.]

Moodie, R.L. 1923. *Paleopathology: An Introduction to the Study of Ancient Evidences of Disease.* University of Illinois Press, Urbana, IL. pp. 38–9, 46–7, 61–78, 80–87, 91–97, 370–371, 402–403, 411, 434–435, 545–557.

Morada, H. 1968. "Postmortem pulmonary edema." *Arch. Pathol.* 85: 468–474.

Motter, M.C. 1898. "A contribution to the study of the fauna of the grave. A study of one hundred and fifty disinterments, with some additional experimental observations." *Journal of the New York Enthomological Society* 6: 201–231.

Mouchacca, J. 1977. "Les champignons de la momie de Ramses II." *C.R. Acad.* (Paris) 285: 515–517.

——. 1978. "Elements biodeteriogenes de la momie de Ramses II." *Bull. Soc. Mycol. Med.* 7: 5–10.

Murad, T.A., Boddy, M.A. 1987. "A case with bear facts." *Journal of Forensic Sciences* 32: 1819–1826.

Murdock, G.P. 1934. *Our Primitive Contemporaries.* New York: MacMillian.

———. 1967. "Ethnographic Atlas: A Summary." *Ethnology* 6: 109–236.

Naipal, Shiva. 1981. "Taking shelter in Bombay." *Geo.* 3 (9): 58–81.

Nehring, J.R., et al. 1972. "Possibility of post-mortem bacterial transmigration." *Arch. Pathol.* 93: 266–270.

Nehring, J.R., Sheridan, M.F., Funk, W.F., Anderson, G.L. 1971. "Studies in post-mortem bacteriology. I. Necropsy Sterility in three patients as long as thirty-five days post-mortem." *Am. J. Clin. Path.* 55: 12–16.

Nielsen, O.V. 1970. "Malignant bone tumors"; p. 116, in Human Remains: Metrical and Non-metrical Anatomical Variations. *The Scandinavian Joint Expedition to Sudanese Nubia,* Vol. 9.

Noe-Nygaard, N. 1977. "Butchering and marrow fracturing as a taphonomic factor in archaeologic deposits." *Paleobiology* 3: 218–237.

Novello, A. 1981. "Rilievi di paleopatologia sullo scheletro della Tomba 5 di San Cesario"; p. 187–188, in *II Neolithic e l'Eta del Rame-Ricerca a Spiamberto.* Cassa di Risparmio di Vignola, Bologna.

Oiso, T. 1975. "Incidence of stomach cancer and its relation to dietary habits and nutrition in Japan between 1900 and 1975." *Cancer Research* 35: 3254–3258.

Olsen, S.J. 1978. "Archaeologically, What Consitutes an Early Domestic Animal?" In *Schiffer,* pp. 175–ff.

Ortner, D.J., Utermohle, C.J. 1981. "Polyarticular inflammatory arthritis in a pre-Columbian skeleton from Kodiak Island, Alaska, USA." *Am. J. Phys. Anthro.* 56: 23–32.

O'Toole, W.F., Saxena, H.M.K., Golden, A., Ritts, R.E. 1965. "Studies of post-mortem microbiology using sterile autopsy technique." *Arch. Path.* 80: 540–547.

Pales, L. 1930. *Paleopathologie et Pathologie Comparative.* Paris: Masson, 352 pages.

Park, E. 1988. "Around the mall and beyond," *Smithsonian* 19 (3): 22–26.

Pastron, A.G., Clewlow, C.W. 1974. "Ethnoarchaeologic Observations on Human Burial Decomposition in the Chihuahua Sierra." In *Ethnoarchaeology,* ed. C. B. Donnan and C. W. Clewlow, Mono. 4. Los Angeles: Institute of Archaeology, University of California. pp. 177–181.

Payne, J.A. 1965. "A summer carrion study of the baby pig sus scrofa linnaeus." *Ecology* 46: 592–602.

———, Crossley, O.J. 1966. *Animal Species Associated with Pig Carrion.* Oak Ridge, Oak Ridge National Library. ORNL–TM–432, 70 pp.

———, King, R.E., Beinhart, G. 1968. "Arthropod succession and decomposition of buried pigs." *Nature* (London) 219: 1180–1181.

Payne, S. 1972. "On the Interpretation of Bone Samples from Archaeologic Sites." In *Papers in Economic Prehistory,* Higgs (ed.), Cambridge, pp. 65–81.

Peck, W.H. 1980. "Mummies of Ancient Egypt" in Cockburn and Cockburn, pp. 10–28.

Perkins, D., Daly, P. 1968. "The potential of faunal analysis: an investigation of faunal remains from Suberde, Turkey." *Scientific American* 219, pp. 96–106.

Petty, G.L. 1969. "The Macleay Museum mummy from Torres Strait: a postscript to Elliot-Smith on the diffussion controversy." *Man.* 4: 24–43.

Polunin, I.V. 1967. "Health and disease in contemporary primitive societies", in *Brothwell and Sandison,* pp. 69–94.

Post, P.W. Donner, D.D. 1972. "Frostbite in a Pre-Columbian mummy." *Amer. J. Phys. Anthro.* 37: 187–192.

Potts, R., Walker, A. 1981. "Production of early hominid archaeological sites." *Amer. J. Phys. Anthro.* 54: 264.

Rathje, W. L. 1982. "Modern material culture studies. In Schiffer, M. B. (ed.) *Advances in Archaeological Method and Theory:* Selections from Vol. 1–4, New York: Academic Press.

Redman, C.L., Watson, P.J. 1970. "Systematic intensive surface collection." *American Antiquity* 35: 279–291.

Reed, H.B. 1958. "A study of dog carcass communities in Tennessee with special reference to the insects." *Am. Midl. Nat.* 59: 213–245.

Riddle, J.M. 1985. "Ancient and medieval chemotherapy for cancer." *ISIS* 75: 319–330.

Ritchie, W.A., Warren, S.L. 1932. "The occurence of multiple bony lesions suggesting myeloma in the skeleton of a pre-Columbian indian." *Am. J. Roentgenol.* 28: 622.

Rivers, W.H.R. 1927. *Medicine, Magic and Religion.* London: Kegan, Paul, Trench, & Trubner.

Rodriguez, W.C., Bass, W.M. 1985. "Decomposition of buried bodies and methods that may aid in their location. *Journal of Forensic Sciences* 30: 836–852.

Rodriguez, W.C., Bass, W.M. 1983. "Insect activity and its relationship to decay rates of human cadavers in East Tennessee." *Journal of Forensic Sciences* 28: 423–430.

Rogers, L. 1949. "Meningiomas in Pharaoh's people: Hypersotosis in ancient Egyptian skulls." *Brit. J. Surg.* 36: 423–434.

Rowling, J.T. 1961. "Pathological changes in mummies." *Proc. Royal Soc. Med.* 54: 409–415.

Rudenko, S.I. 1970. *Frozen Tombs of Siberia.* Edited and translated by M.W. Thompson. Berkeley: University of California Press.

Ruffer, M.A. 1921. *Studies in the Paleopathology of Egypt.* University of Chicago Press, Chicago.

Ruffer, M.A., Willmore, J.G. 1914. Studies in paleopathology: Note on a tumor of the pelvis dating from Roman times (250 A.D.) and found in Egypt. *J. Pathol. Bacteriol.* 18: 480–484.

Rust, A.L. 1943. *Die Alt- und Mittelsteinzeitlichen Funde von Stellmoor.* Neunmunster: Karl Wachholtz.

Salama, N., Hilmy, A. 1950. "A case of an osteogenic sarcoma of the maxilla in an ancient Egyptian skull." *Brit. Dent. J.* 88: 101–102.

Sandison, A.T. 1970. "The study of mummified and dried human tissues," in Brothwell, D.R. and Higgs, E. (eds.), *Science in Archaeology,* 2nd ed., Praeger, New York.

Sandison, A.T. 1975. "Kanam mandible's tumour." *Lancet* 1: 279.

Sandison, A.T. 1980. "Diseases in ancient Egypt", in *Cockburn and Cockburn,* pp. 29–44.

Satinoff, A.T. Report of Seventeenth Tagung der Gesellschaft fur Arthropologie und Humangenetik. *Paleopathology Newsletter* 37: 5–6.

Satinoff, M.J. 1968. "Preliminary report on the paleopathology of collection of ancient Egyptian skeletons." *Rivista di Antropologia* 55: 41–50.

Satinoff, M.J., Wells, C. 1969. "Multiple basal cell naevus syndrome in ancient Egypt." *Med. History* 13: 294–297.

Saul, F.P., Micozzi, M.S. 1988. "The identification of fleshed remains: the changing role of the forensic anthropologist. I." Annual Meeting, *American Academy of Forensic Sciences,* Philadelphia, PA, p. 108.

Saul, F.P., Micozzi, M.S. 1989. "The identification of fleshed remains: the changing role of the forensic anthropologist. II." *American Academy of Forensic Sciences,* Las Vegas, NV, p. 118.

Sauneron, S. 1952. *Ritual de l'Embaumement, Papier Boulag 3, Papier Louvre* 5, 158. Service des Antiquities de l'Egypt, Caire.

Schiffer, Michael B. 1972. "Archaeologic Context and Systemic context." *American Antiquity* 37: 256–265.

——. 1976. *Behavioral Archaeology.* New York: Academic Press.

Schoof, H.F., Savaga, E.P., Dodge, H.R. 1956. "Comparative studies of urban fly populations in Arizona, Kansas, Michigan, New York and West Virginia II. Seasonal abundance of minor species." *Ann. Entomol. Soc. Am.* 48: 59–66.

Schultz, A.H. 1967. "Notes on diseases and healed fractures of wild apes," in *Brothwell and Sandison,* p. 47.

Service, E.R. 1958. *A Profile of Primitive Culture.* New York: Harper.

Shafer. 1978. *The Ecology and Paleoecology of Marine Environments.* Chicago: University of Chicago Press.

Shanklin, D.R. 1972. "Post-mortem bacterial transmigration." *Arch. Pathol.* 94: 197 (letter).

Sharer, J., Ashmore, W. 1979. *Fundamentals of Archaeology.* Menlo Park, Ca.: Benjamin Cummings.

Shipman, P. 1975. "Implications of drought for vertebrate faunal assemblages." *Nature* 257: 667–668.

Sigerist, H.E. 1951. *A History of Medicine,* Vol. I: Primitive and Archaic Medicine. New York; Oxford University Press, pp. 58–59.

Sluglett, J. 1981. "Mummification in Ancient Egypt." *MASCA Journal* I: 163–167.

Smith, G.S., Zimmermann, M.R. 1975. "Tattooing Found on 1600 Year Old Frozen, Mummified Body from St. Lawrence Island, Alaska." *Am Antiq.* 40: 434–437.

Soulie, R. 1980. "New evidence for skull metastasis of malignant neoplasm in the European Bronze Age." Papers on Paleopathology presented at the Third European Members Meeting of the Paleopathology Association, Caen, France, September.

Spielman, P.E. 1932. "To what extent did the ancient Egyptian employ bitumen for embalming?" *J. of Egyptian Arch.* 18: 177–180.

Stannard, David E. 1975. *Death in America.* Philadelphia: University of Pennsylvania Press.

——. 1977. *The Puritan Way of Death: A Story in Religion, Culture and Social Change.* Oxford: Oxford University Press.

Stead, I.M., Bourke, J.B., Brothwell, D. 1986. *Lindow Man: The Body in the Bog.* New York: Cornell University Press.

Steinbock, R.T. 1976. *Paleopathological Diagnosis and Interpretation: Bone Diseases in Ancient Human Populations.* Springfield, IL; Charles C Thomas, 422 pages.

Steinbock, R.T. 1988. Annotated Bibliography. *Paleopathology Newsletter* 62: 11, (abstract).

Steinfeld, A.D., McDuff, H.C. 1980. "An ancient report of a dermoid cyst of the vagina." *Surg. Gyn. Obstet.* 150: 95–96.

Stewart, W. 1907. *John Paul Jones. Commemoration at* Annapolis, April 24, 1906. Washington: U.S. Government Printing Office.

Stewart, T.D. 1979. *Essentials of Forensic Anthropology.* Springfield, IL; Charles C Thomas.

Strouhal, E. 1976. "Tumours in the remains of ancient Egyptians." *Am. J. Phys. Anthro.* 45: 613–620.

Strouhal, E. 1978. "Ancient Egyptian case of carcinoma [nasopharyngeal]." *Bull NY. Acad. Med.* 54. pp. 290–302.

Sulzer, A. 1981. Letter. *Paleopathology Newsletter* 36: 9–10.

Suraiya, J.N. 1973. "Medicine in ancient India with special reference to cancer." *Indian Journal of Cancer* 10: 391–402.

Sutcliffe, A.J. 1970. "Spotted hyena: crusher, gnawer, digestor and collector of bones." *Nature* 227: 1110–1113.

———. 1973. "Similarity of bones and antlers gnawed by deer to human artifacts." *Nature* 246: 248–430.

Swinton, W.E. 1983. "Animal Paleopathology: Its Relation to Ancient Human Disease." In Hart, G.D., (ed): *Disease in Ancient Man.* Clarke Irwin, Toronto; pp. 50–58.

Tainter, J.A. 1978. "Mortuary Practices and the Study of Prehistoric Social Systems." In *Schiffer,* M. B., pp. 106–143.

Taylor, N.W. 1964. "Tethered Nomadism and Territoriality: An Hypothesis" *Acts of the 35th Int. Cong. of Americanists,* pp. 197–203. Mexico City.

Thomas, D. H. 1971. "On distinguishing natural from cultural bone in archaeologic sites." *American Antiquity* 36: 366–371.

Tkocz, I., Bytzer, P., Bierring, F. 1979. "Preserved brains in medieval skulls." *Am. J. Phys. Anthro.* 51: 197–202.

Toots, H. 1965. "Sequence of disarticulation in mammalian skeletons." *University of Wyoming Contributions in Geology* 4 (1): 37–39.

Torre, C., Giacobini, G., Sicuro, A. 1980. "The skull and vertebral column pathology of ancient Egyptians. A Study of the Marro Colletion." *J. Human Evolution* 9: 41–44.

Ubelaker, D.H. 1974. "Reconstruction of demographic profiles from ossuary skeletal samples." *Smithsonian Contributions to Anthropology,* No. 18. Smithsonian Institution Press.

Ubelaker, D.H. "The Development of American Paleopathology," in Spencer, F. (ed), *A History of American Physical Anthropology,* 1930–1980, Academic Press, 1982; pp. 337–356.

Ubelaker, D.H. 1989. *Human Skeletal Remains: Excavation, Analysis, Interpretation,* 2nd ed., Washington, D.C.: Taraxacum Press.

Urteaga, O.B., Pack, G.T. 1966. "On the antiquity of melanoma." *Cancer* 19: 607–610.

U.S. Department of Health and Human Services, PHS, NIH, *Closing in on Cancer.* NIH Publication No. 87-2955, September; 1987.

Van Houten, T. 1980a,b. The Edwin Smith papyrus: I. The surgical management of cranial injuries. II. Surgical management in cases of uncertain or dubious prognosis. *Museum Appl. Sci. Cntr. for Anthropol* (MASCA) Journal 1: 99–101, 182–184.

Vignati, M.A. 1930. "Los craneous trofeo." *Archives del Museo Ethnografico,* Numero 1. Buenos Aires.

Virchow, R. 1870. "Knochen wom Hohlenbaren mit krankhaften Veranderungen." *Z. Ethnol,* Bd. 2, p. 365, footnote.

——. 1895. "Ueber einen Besuch der westfallischen Knochenhohle." *Z. Ethnol.,* Bd. 27; pp. 706–708, Figs. 1–4.

——. "Beitrag zur geschichte der lues." *Dermat Z,* Bd 3, p.4.

Vrba, E.S. 1975. "Some evidence of chronology and paleoecology at Sterkfontein, Swartkraans and Kromdraii from the fossil bovidae." *Nature* 254: 301–304.

——. 1980. "The Significance of Bovid Remains as Indicators of Environment and Predation Patterns." In *Behernsmeyer and Hill,* pp. 247–271.

Vreeland, J. 1978. "Prehistoric Andean Mortuary Practices: Preliminary Report from Peru." *Current Anthropology* 19: 212–213.

Voorhies, M.R. 1969. "Taphonomy and Population Dynamics of Early Pliocene Vertebrate Fauna, Knox County, Nebraska." *University of Wyoming Contributions to Geology,* Special Paper No. 1, 69 pp.

Wada, Y., Ikeda, J., Suzuki, T. (1987) "Tumor-like lesions in a human skeleton from the Himrin basin of Iraq," *J. Anthrop. Soc. Nippon* 95: 107–119.

Waisbard, S., Waisbard, R. 1965. *Masks, Mummies and Magicians.* London: Oliver and Boyd.

Walker, P.L., Long, J.C. 1977. "An experimental study of the morphological characteristics of tooth marks." *American Antiquity* 42: 605–616.

Wallace, Alfred Russel. 1869. The Malay Archipelago: *The Land of the Orang Utan and the Greater Bird of Paradise.* London: Macmillan.

Warren, C.P. 1975. "Plants as decomposition vectors of human skeletal remains." *Indiana Academy of Sciences,* 91st Annual Meeting, Butler University.

Warren, C.P. 1980. "Plants and related decomposition vectors of human skeletal remains." Abstract, *American Academy of Forensic Sciences,* 32nd Annual Meeting, New Orleans, LA. p. 97.

Wells, C. 1963. Ancient Egyptian pathology. *J. Laryngol Otol.* 77: 261–265.

Wells, C. 1964. *Bones, Bodies and Disease.* London; Thames & Hudson, pp. 70–76.

Wells, C. 1964. "Two medieval cases of malignant disease." *Brit. Med. J.* 1: 16.

Weigelt, J. 1927. *Resente Wirbeltlierleichen und Ihre Paleobiologische Bedeutung.* Leipzig: Verlag von Max Weg.

Weisberger, E.K. 1979. "Natural carcinogenic compounds." *Environmental Science and Technology* 13: 278–281.

Williams, G.D., Ritchie, W.A., Titterington, D.F. 1941. "Multiple bony lesions suggesting myeloma in pre-columbian Indian aged ten years." *Am J. Roentgenol.* 46: 351.

Williams, H.U. 1929. "Human Paleopathology." *Arch. Pathol.* 7: 839–902.

Wilson, W.R., Dolan, C.T., Washington, J.A., Brown, A.L., Ritts, R.E. 1972. "Clinical significance of post-mortem cultures." *Arch. Path.* 94: 244–249.

Wolberg, D.L. 1970. "The hypothesized osteodontokeratic culture of the Australopithecines: a look at the evidence and the opinion." *Current Anthropology* 11: 23–27.

Wood, W.R., Johnson, D.L. 1978. "A Survey of Disturbance Process in Archaeological Site Formation." In Schiffer, pp. 315–383.

Yellen, J. E. 1977. "Cultural Patterning in Faunal Remains: Evidence from the Kung Bushmen." In *Experimental Archaeology,* edited by D. Ingersoll, J. E. Yellen and M. MacDonald. New York: Columbia U. Press. pp. 271–331.

Zammit, T. Singer, C. 1924. "Neolithic representations of the human form from the Islands of Malta and Gozo." *J. Royal Anthro. Inst.* 54: 67.

Zimmerman, M.R. 1972. "Histological examination of experimentally mummified tissues." *Am. J. Phys. Anthropol.* 37: 271–280.

Zimmerman, M.R. 1976. "A Paleopathologic and Archaeologic Investigation of the Human Remains of the Dra Abu el-Naga Site, Egypt: Based on an Experimental Study of Mummification." Ph.D. Thesis, University of Pennsylvania, PA.

Zimmerman, M.R. 1977. "An experimental study of mummification pertinent to the antiquity of cancer." *Cancer* 40: 1358–1362.

INDEX

S

Salt
    preservation by, 10
    water, 58
Saltpeter, 10
Sampling, 4–5
Saponification (*see* Adipocere)
Scavengers
    studies, 8
    vs. predators, 59–61
Sea birds, 6
Sea mammals, 6
Shrunken heads, 10, 20
Siberia, 12
Skin
    and bone, 57
    natron effects on, 27
    preservation of, 9–10, 12
    tattoos, 12
Smithsonian Institution, 19, 31, 46,
        101
South America, 20–21
Southeast Asia, 22
Southeast U.S., 10–11
Southern California, 19
Southwest U.S., 9–10, 51–52
Stoll-McCracken Expedition, 19
Symbolism, 15–16

T

Tannic acid (Tannins), 12, 21, 34
Taphocoenose, 3–4
Taphonomy
    definition, 3
    and forensic pathology, 5–6
    studies, 6–7

Tau-tau, 22
Tempura cooking, 34
Tetracycline, 34
Tibet, 21
Time interval
        since death, 4–5
        studies, 5–6
Transylvania, 96
Tsanta, 21

U

Uganda, 66

V

Vinca, 97
Virginia, 19, 51
Vultures, 21, 60

W

Wallace, Alfred Russel, 22
Western Pacific, 23–24
Wyoming, 6

X

X, histiocytosis-, 92, 100–101
X-ray, 98

Y

Yugoslavia, 97, 101

Z

Zambia, 60, 62–63
Zoroastrianism, 21